P9-CFO-385

# TRAVEL GAMES

Publications International, Ltd.

Images from Shutterstock.com and Wikimedia Commons

**Brain Games is a registered trademark of Publications International, Ltd.**

Copyright © 2018 Publications International, Ltd. All rights reserved. This book may not be reproduced or quoted in whole or in part by any means whatsoever without written permission from:

Louis Weber, CEO
Publications International, Ltd.
8140 Lehigh Avenue
Morton Grove, IL 60053

Permission is never granted for commercial purposes.

ISBN: 978-1-64030-113-9

Manufactured in China.

8 7 6 5 4 3 2 1

# TABLE OF CONTENTS

## BINGO

Travel Bingo combines a scavenger hunt and the classic Bingo game into a fun activity perfect for family trips. The boards are made up of 5 vertical columns and 5 horizontal rows with one free space in the center. The object of the game is to cover 5 squares in a vertical, horizontal, or diagonal row. Use the Bingo boards found on pages 8–15 and give one to each player. When player finds an item on their board, the player covers the item with a coin or similar object. The first player with a full row (vertical, horizontal, or diagonal) says "Bingo!" to win.

If you don't have coins, bottle caps, or similar objects to cover the board squares, you can use a pencil mark on the square. If there is only one player, the object of the game is to cover all of the squares on the board.

## TIC TAC TOE

Tic Tac Toe is a two-player game. All you need are two players, pencils, and one of the 3 x 3 grids on pages 16–19 to play. Each player chooses their form—either an X or an O. The players take turns marking their X or O in the grid. The players continue taking turns until one player succeeds in having three in a horizontal, vertical, or diagonal row. That player wins the game. As a variation, players can select a shape as their form to draw in the grid spaces rather than an X or an O.

## CONNECT THE DOTS

Connect the Dots is a two-player game. You need two different colored pencils, pens, crayons, or markers and one of the Connect the Dots grids on pages 20–23. The first player draws a straight line between two adjacent dots with their colored pencil, pen, crayon, or marker. You can use any dots on the page, but the lines must be vertical or horizontal. No diagonal lines are allowed. The second player does the same with a different color. The goal is to create a box with four enclosed sides. Each time a box is created, the player who completed the box puts their initials in the box. The player who creates the most boxes wins the game.

## HANGMAN

Hangman is a two-player game. You can start with one of the Hangman templates on pages 24–29. The first player thinks of a word, phrase, name, or title, and draws a space (an underline or box) for each letter. The second player guesses one letter at a time. If the mystery word or phrase contains that letter, it is written in the correct place(s). If not, the first player draws a head on the hangman and continues to draw parts of that body for each wrong letter guessed. The game is over when the mystery word or phrase is completed or guessed, or when the hangman body is complete.

## LICENSE PLATE GAME

Use one of the License Plate Game sheets from pages 30–34. Every time a player sees a license plate from a state on their sheet, the player covers or crosses it off. The first player to find all the plates on their sheet wins the game.

## 20 QUESTIONS

This classic guessing game is for two or more players. The first player begins by thinking of a person, place, or thing. The other players take turns guessing the mystery person, place, or thing by asking questions that can be answered with a "yes" or a "no." Keep asking questions until 20 questions have been asked and answered. At any time, the players can guess what the person, place, or thing is. The player who guesses correctly then becomes the person thinking up the mystery item in the next round. If nobody guesses correctly after 20 questions, the first player wins and thinks up another item in the next round.

## ALPHABET GAME

The Alphabet Game is a search game with two or more players. The first player looks around for something that begins with the letter A. For example, *automobile*, *avenue*, or *airplane*. The next player then looks around for something visible to everyone that begins with the letter B, like *bike*,

*bus*, or *bridge*. The game continues until the players have gone through the entire alphabet. For tricky letters, players can use license plates containing those letters.

## I SPY

I Spy is a guessing game for two or more players. To play I Spy, one player says, "I spy with my little eye something…" and gives a clue to about the thing they have spotted, which should be visible to all players. The other players take turns guessing what the mystery item is. Good clues to give can be the color, the beginning letter or sound, something it rhymes with, or its shape. The player who guesses correctly wins.

## SIMON SAYS

This group game is best played in settings where the players have some room. One player is selected to be Simon. Simon tells the other players what to do. But the players must only follow commands that begin with the words "Simon says." So, "Simon says touch your knee," would be a valid command, but just "touch your knee" would not be, and following it would get you kicked out.

# BINGO

| | | | | |
|---|---|---|---|---|
| STOP | R×R | traffic light | keep right | SPEED LIMIT 55 |
| workers | NO U-TURN | DO NOT PASS | slippery | NO PEDESTRIAN CROSSING |
| motorcycle | hill | FREE | DO NOT ENTER | truck |
| winding road | P | SPEED LIMIT 45 | tow truck | NO PARKING ANY TIME |
| YIELD | U-turn | RAIL ROAD CROSSING | no trucks | merge |

# BINGO

15

# TIC TAC TOE

# CONNECT THE DOTS

# CONNECT THE DOTS

# CONNECT THE DOTS

# HANGMAN

_____

A    B    C    D    E    F    G    H    I
   J    K    L    M    N    O    P    Q
R    S    T    U    V    W    X    Y    Z

# HANGMAN

_____

A   B   C   D   E   F   G   H   I
  J   K   L   M   N   O   P   Q
R   S   T   U   V   W   X   Y   Z

# HANGMAN

_____

A   B   C   D   E   F   G   H   I

  J   K   L   M   N   O   P   Q

R   S   T   U   V   W   X   Y   Z

# HANGMAN

_____

A   B   C   D   E   F   G   H   I

J   K   L   M   N   O   P   Q

R   S   T   U   V   W   X   Y   Z

# HANGMAN

_____

A   B   C   D   E   F   G   H   I

  J   K   L   M   N   O   P   Q

R   S   T   U   V   W   X   Y   Z

# HANGMAN

_____

A    B    C    D    E    F    G    H    I

J    K    L    M    N    O    P    Q

R    S    T    U    V    W    X    Y    Z

# LICENSE PLATE GAME

TENNESSEE

FLORIDA

GEORGIA

ARKANSAS

TEXAS

MISSISSIPPI

VIRGINIA

KANSAS

KENTUCKY

NORTH
CAROLINA

NEVADA

COLORADO

MONTANA

PENNSYLVANIA

SOUTH
DAKOTA

# LICENSE PLATE GAME

TEXAS

WISCONSIN

NEBRASKA

ILLINOIS

MINNESOTA

MICHIGAN

TENNESSEE

KENTUCKY

IDAHO

MISSISSIPPI

MISSOURI

NEW YORK

OHIO

DELAWARE

MASSACHUSETTS

# LICENSE PLATE GAME

ALASKA

CALIFORNIA

NEW MEXICO

NEVADA

COLORADO

WEST
VIRGINIA

NEBRASKA

WASHINGTON

DISTRICT OF
COLUMBIA

ARIZONA

MONTANA

FLORIDA

NEW JERSEY

HAWAII

MAINE

# LICENSE PLATE GAME

MAINE

MICHIGAN

MASSACHUSETTS

MARYLAND

MONTANA

MINNESOTA

MISSISSIPPI

MISSOURI

NEBRASKA

NEVADA

NEW JERSEY

NEW MEXICO

NORTH
CAROLINA

NEW YORK

NEW HAMPSHIRE

33

# LICENSE PLATE GAME

**NEW JERSEY**

**PENNSYLVANIA**

**CONNECTICUT**

**NEW YORK**

**MAINE**

**DELAWARE**

**MASSACHUSETTS**

**VERMONT**

**SOUTH CAROLINA**

**NEW HAMPSHIRE**

**VIRGINIA**

**NORTH CAROLINA**

**MARYLAND**

**DISTRICT OF COLUMBIA**

**GEORGIA**

# TRIVIA QUESTIONS

**1.** What is the biggest city (by population) in North America?

    A. Toronto
    B. New York City
    C. Mexico City
    D. Los Angeles

**2.** What is the most remote island in the world?

    A. Saint Helena
    B. Bouvet Island
    C. Easter Island
    D. Kiribati

**3.** What European capital is home to more dogs than people?

    A. London
    B. Berlin
    C. Paris
    D. Amsterdam

**4.** True or false: The Dead Sea is the world's saltiest body of water.

**1. C.** With a population of 8.9 million, Mexico City beats out all the competition.

- *In 2013, Toronto (population 2.79 million) overtook Chicago to become the fourth-largest city in North America.*

**2. B.** This South Atlantic island is almost a thousand miles away from its closest neighbor, Queen Maude Land, Antarctica. If you need to borrow a cup of sugar, though, you're out of luck—the island is uninhabited.

**3. C.** When visiting the French capital, *attention à la marche* (watch your step).

**4. False:** The Dead Sea's salinity is 340 grams per liter, but Lake Asal in the East African country of Djibouti blows that out of the water with a salinity of 400 grams per liter. But before you think about bobbing in its curative waters, keep in mind that Lake Asal has a salt crust up to 13 inches thick along its "shore"— thick enough to drive a car on!

**5.** Which is the largest continent?
>A. North America
>B. Antarctica
>C. Africa
>D. Asia

**6.** What is the only one of the seven wonders of the ancient world still in existence?

**7.** What is the capital of Turkey?
>A. Ankara
>B. Istanbul
>C. Bursa
>D. Adana

**8.** The deepest area in the world's oceans shares a name with which space shuttle?
>A. *Atlantis*
>B. *Challenger*
>C. *Columbia*
>D. *Discovery*

# TRIVIA ANSWERS

**5. D.** Asia is the largest continent both by land mass (44,579,000 square miles) and population (4.4 billion).

**6. The Great Pyramid of Giza.** The other six wonders—the Colossus of Rhodes, the Hanging Gardens of Babylon, the lighthouse at Alexandria, the mausoleum at Halicarnassus, the statue of Zeus at Olympia, and the Temple of Artemis at Ephesus—are lost to the sands of time.

**7. A.** This planned city beat out its big sister Istanbul because of its position right in the center of the country—much to the Turkish delight of its residents!

**8. B.** Challenger Deep is named after the ship HMS *Challenger* whose crew discovered the depth—nearly seven miles!—of this part of the Pacific Ocean.

# TRIVIA QUESTIONS

**9.** Which South American country is home to the ancient city of Machu Picchu?

       A. Brazil
       B. Colombia
       C. Bolivia
       D. Peru

**10.** Amsterdam is sometimes called the "Venice of the North." How many canals does it have?

       A. 55
       B. 105
       C. 165
       D. 215

**11.** What is the only country with a flag that is *not* rectangular or square?

       A. Yemen
       B. Nepal
       C. Switzerland
       D. Mexico

**12.** Which landmark shrinks about six inches every winter?

       A. Big Ben
       B. Leaning Tower of Pisa
       C. Eiffel Tower
       D. Giralda Tower

# TRIVIA ANSWERS

**9. D.** The ancient home of the Inca Empire used to be a six-day walk from civilization, but now train travelers can leave from Cusco, Peru, and arrive in mere hours.

- *Even without mortar, the stones that make up the citadel of Machu Picchu fit together so tightly that even a knife blade won't fit in the seams.*

**10. C.** And along with the canals are 1,281 bridges, most of which open to let ships pass through and provide Dutch schoolchildren with a handy "The bridge was open" excuse for tardiness. Hey, it beats "The dog ate my homework."

**11. B.** Nepal's flag is made of two joined triangular shapes with sun and moon designs.

- *Switzerland and Vatican City are the only countries with square flags.*

**12. C.** Like a swimmer in cold water, the metal tower is susceptible to temperature-induced shrinkage.

**13.** Where is the Colosseum located?

     A. Athens
     B. Florence
     C. Jerusalem
     D. Rome

**14.** In what Spanish city does the famous "running of the bulls" festival take place each July?

     A. Barcelona
     B. Madrid
     C. Pamplona
     D. Valencia

**15.** The United States has shoreline on how many oceans?

**16.** Take a trip to Easter Island and you'll find yourself vacationing with which magnificent statues?

     A. 4,012 Golems
     B. 887 Moai
     C. 263 Koias
     D. 8,045 Sirhc

**13. D.** The arena was built in A.D. 80 and was primarily a venue where Romans enjoyed the spectacles of gladiator battles and wild animal fights.

**14. C.** Olé! Unlike bullfights, which are open only to professionals, anyone age 18 or older is welcome to participate in the *encierro* (running of the bulls).

**15. Three:** Atlantic, Pacific, and Arctic.

**16. B.** Easter Island, a Polynesian island in the Pacific Ocean, is home to 887 statues known as Moai. They were created by the Rapa Nui people and are found mostly near the coasts of Rapa Nui, the Polynesian name for the island. Easter Island can rightfully be called the middle of nowhere; the closest inhabited island is more than 1,200 miles away, and that island only has 50 permanent residents.

**17.** True or false: There are two European countries that are smaller than New York City's Central Park.

**18.** Lake Baikal, the deepest lake on Earth, is located within which continent?
- A. Asia
- B. Europe
- C. Africa
- D. Australia

**19.** What's the only city in the world that's located on two continents?
- A. Cairo, Egypt
- B. Anchorage, Alaska, U.S.A.
- C. Ceuta, Spain
- D. Istanbul, Turkey

**20.** On September 3, 1967, Sweden switched sides—which side of the road do drivers drive on now?

**17. True.** Central Park covers 1.3 square miles, while Monaco covers 0.7 square miles and the tiny nation of Vatican City only occupies 0.2 square miles.

**18. A.** Cold, cold, COLD Lake Baikal is found in Siberia, with basins in both Russia and Mongolia. It's not only the deepest lake on the planet, but also Earth's clearest and most voluminous freshwater lake, accounting for more than 20 percent of the world's unfrozen surface freshwater. And it's thought to be the world's oldest lake, having been around for approximately 25 million years.

**19. D.** Istanbul, Turkey. Istanbul flanks the Bosporus Strait between Asia and Europe. (See, all those years of studying for the National Geographic Geography Bee finally paid off!)

**20. The right.** Just before 5 A.M. there was a brief countrywide traffic jam as all traffic stopped and switched sides before heading off to start the workday.

# TRIVIA QUESTIONS

**21.** In which Southern U.S. state can you find the towns Republican and Democrat?

  A. North Carolina
  B. Georgia
  C. South Carolina
  D. Arkansas

**22.** This'll perk you right up! Which of these is *not* a real town named after America's favorite caffeinated beverage?

  A. Hot Coffee, Mississippi
  B. Coffeeville, Alabama
  C. Coffee Creek, Montana
  D. Coffee Cup, Washington

**23.** What is the official language of Brazil?

  A. English
  B. French
  C. Portuguese
  D. Spanish

**24.** Where is Stonehenge?

  A. England
  B. Ireland
  C. Scotland
  D. Wales

**21. A.** Though each party is known for digging in its Tar Heels when debate season rolls around.

**22. D.** But it's a great sponsorship opportunity for Starbucks!

**23. C.** Brazil is the only nation in South America whose official language is Portuguese. Most of the other South American countries claim Spanish as their national language, although French (French Guiana), English (Guyana), and Dutch (Suriname) also make the list.

**24. A.** Okay, we know *where* the prehistoric monument is (Wiltshire County, southwest England), but do we know *what* it is? Not really. The best guesses include a temple for sun worship, a healing center, a burial site, and a huge calendar.

## TRIVIA QUESTIONS

**25.** In which hand does the Statue of Liberty hold a torch?

**26.** How many spikes are there in the Statue of Liberty's crown and what do they represent?

**27.** Which river flows through the Grand Canyon?
     A. Colorado
     B. Columbia
     C. Green
     D. Rio Grande

**28.** Hawaii has eight major islands. How many can you name?

**25. Right.** In the statue's left hand is a tablet inscribed with the date July IV MDCCLXXVI—July 4, 1776—to commemorate American independence.

- *The current torch is actually the second for Lady Liberty. The first was removed in 1984 and can be seen up close and personal on display in the Pedestal lobby.*

**26. Seven.** Lady Liberty's spikes symbolize the seven seas.

**27. A.** The Colorado River is the Southwest's longest river. It begins in the Rocky Mountains in Colorado and flows almost 1,500 miles before emptying into the Gulf of California in Mexico.

**28.** They are Hawaii (the Big Island), Kahoolawe, Kauai, Lanai, Maui, Molokai, Niihau, and Oahu.

**29.** In what country is the world's tallest building?

    A. Malaysia
    B. Qatar
    C. China
    D. United Arab Emirates

**30.** What is the longest river in the world?

    A. Amazon
    B. Mississippi
    C. Nile
    D. Yangtze

**31.** What is the smallest country in the world?

    A. Liechtenstein
    B. Monaco
    C. Nauro
    D. Vatican City

**32.** Where is the only place that the American flag flies continuously and is never raised or lowered?

**29.** **D.** At 2,722.57 feet, the Burj Khalifa in Dubai, UAE, is the tallest man-made structure in the world. It was completed in 2010.

- *The Burj Khalifa may soon relinquish its title. If completed in 2020 as planned, the Jeddah Tower in Saudi Arabia will surpass the Burj Khalifa.*

**30.** **C.** At 4,132 miles long, the Nile, which starts in Lake Victoria and flows north through Africa all the way to the Mediterranean Sea, is more than 100 miles longer than its closest competitor (the Amazon, in South America).

**31.** **D.** At just 0.2 square miles in area, the tiny country has a population of less than 800 people. It is surrounded by Rome and is the spiritual center of Roman Catholicism.

**32.** **The moon.**

**33.** Before it was settled in Washington, D.C., the U.S. capital was in eight other cities. Which of these did *not* serve as the capital?

> A. Philadelphia, Pennsylvania
> B. Montpelier, Vermont
> C. Trenton, New Jersey
> D. Baltimore, Maryland

**34.** Which state extends farthest east?

> A. Maine
> B. Alaska
> C. Rhode Island
> D. Massachusetts

**35.** Which four American presidents appear on Mount Rushmore?

**36.** There's another memorial being carved into a mountain in the Black Hills of South Dakota. Who is the subject of this monument?

> A. Chief Joseph
> B. Crazy Horse
> C. Geronimo
> D. Sitting Bull

**33. B.** Montpelier, Vermont, did not serve as the U.S. capital. Lancaster, Pennsylvania; York, Pennsylvania; Princeton, New Jersey; Annapolis, Maryland; and Manhattan, New York, also took turns as the nation's capital.

**34. A.** Maine extends farthest east.

**35.** George Washington, Thomas Jefferson, Theodore Roosevelt, and Abraham Lincoln.

**36. B.** The Crazy Horse memorial has been under construction since 1948. When it's finally finished it will be the largest statue in the world—more than 600 feet long and almost as tall.

**37.** Lake Michigan touches which states?

    A. Wisconsin and Michigan
    B. Wisconsin, Michigan, Illinois, and Indiana
    C. Only Michigan
    D. Michigan, Ohio, and Pennsylvania

**38.** What is the highest point in the United States?

    A. Mount Rushmore
    B. Empire State Building, New York City
    C. Willis Tower, Chicago
    D. Denali (Mount McKinley)

**39.** Connecticut was the first state to set a speed limit. At what "blazing" speed would cars hit that limit?

    A. 5 miles per hour
    B. 7 miles per hour
    C. 9 miles per hour
    D. 12 miles per hour

**37. B.** Lake Michigan touches four states—Wisconsin, Michigan, Illinois, and Indiana.

**38. D.** Denali, also known as Mount McKinley, is the highest point in the United States with an elevation of 20,310 feet.

**39. D.** Outside of city limits, however, cars could travel at the breakneck pace of 15 miles per hour.

# TRIVIA QUESTIONS

**40.** Where can Io, Europa, Ganymede, and Callisto be found?

**41.** Which American city is known for dying its river green for St. Patrick's Day every year?

A. Chicago
B. Cleveland
C. New Orleans
D. New York City

**40.** **Orbiting Jupiter:** They are the four largest of Jupiter's 66 moons.

**41.** **A.** Although some would argue that the river is always a murky shade of green, 40 pounds of nontoxic vegetable dye transform it into a bright, Irish green for the city's annual St. Paddy's Day parade.

# IT'S A ZOO!

Find the animals hidden in the grid below. Words can be found in a straight line horizontally, vertically, or diagonally. They may read either forward or backward.

APE

ELEPHANT

GIRAFFE

GORILLA

HIPPO

LION

MONKEY

PANDA

TIGER

ZEBRA

```
I  G  T  G  U  X  Q  F  G  E
T  I  G  E  R  Y  K  L  O  Q
N  R  P  X  N  N  K  A  R  K
A  A  C  K  O  X  D  J  I  R
H  F  T  U  L  N  O  I  L  Q
P  F  H  N  A  K  E  Z  L  V
E  E  O  P  P  I  H  C  A  H
L  A  W  B  X  C  O  K  Q  B
E  R  Z  E  B  R  A  Z  E  K
S  G  G  M  O  N  K  E  Y  Q
```

# CROSSWORD

## ACROSS
1. Not good
4. Old cloth used for dusting
7. Go ___ vacation
8. Word ending that means "sort of"
9. It holds back water in a river
12. Strange
13. Enjoy a winter sport
14. Cheer for a bullfighter
15. City in Florida
17. Tokyo's country
19. Number that appears on a penny
21. Geeky person
22. Monkey bars
25. Not straight
26. Distant
27. "Honesty ___ best policy"
29. It's poured over waffles
33. "Just ___ thought!"
34. Struck a match
36. Had a snack
37. "___ you later, alligator!"
38. He runs a bar on *The Simpsons*
39. Sound made by a woodpecker
40. Your and my
41. That lady

## DOWN
1. Sound of an explosion
2. Me, myself, ___
3. How a baby might say "father"
4. Moving up
5. Have a question
6. Letters after F
9. One of the Seven Dwarfs
10. ___ clock (item that can wake you up)
11. Heal
16. $\frac{1}{12}$ of a year
18. Really upset
20. One of Santa's assistants
22. ___ James (famous outlaw)
23. Remove a knot
24. Holiday with bunnies and eggs
25. Prejudice
28. Red Muppet
30. "Darn it!"
31. State with the Great Salt Lake
32. ___ Le Pew (cartoon skunk)
35. Paper that shows a debt

# LOOP-DE-LOOP

Can you loop your way in and out of this maze?

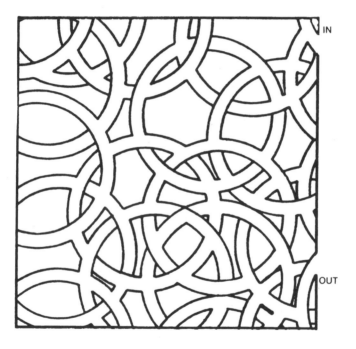

IN

OUT

*Answer on page 229.*

# MOUNTAINS OF FUN

Draw a line from consecutive numbers, starting at
1 and ending at 101, to reveal a winter sport.

# U.S. NATIONAL PARKS

Every word listed is contained within the group
of letters. Words can be found in a straight line
horizontally, vertically, or diagonally. They may
read either forward or backward.

| | |
|---|---|
| ARCHES | MAMMOTH CAVE |
| BADLANDS | MESA VERDE |
| BRYCE CANYON | MOUNT RAINIER |
| CARLSBAD CAVERNS | OLYMPIC |
| CRATER LAKE | SEQUOIA |
| DEATH VALLEY | PETRIFIED FOREST |
| DENALI | WRANGELL-ST. ELIAS |
| EVERGLADES | YELLOWSTONE |
| GLACIER | YOSEMITE |
| GRAND CANYON | ZION |
| GRAND TETON | |
| KINGS CANYON | |

```
C A R L S B A D C A V E R N S
F V B R Y C E C A N Y O N Y Q
E M O U N T R A I N I E R Z I
P E T R I F I E D F O R E S T
I E T I M E S O Y K J S M A N
L Z E N O T S W O L L E Y I O
A Y E L L A V H T A E D C L Y
N G P M A M M O T H C A V E N
E L P G Q J X K C D F L G T A
D A Z X O L Y M P I C G R S C
Z C I Q T E M S I U S R A L S
C I O X M K N J Y E E N L G
G E N S R G W J H N Q V D E N
D R J G B C K C K H U E T G I
M E S A V E R D E Y O Y E N K
J V S D N A L D A B I T T A Z
E K A L R E T A R C A B O R K
F N O Y N A C D N A R G N W Y
```

# CARTOGRAPHY

Every word listed is contained within the group of letters. Words can be found in a straight line horizontally, vertically, or diagonally. They may read either forward or backward.

ATLAS

AZIMUTH

BATHYMETRY

BOUNDARY

CARDINAL DIRECTIONS

CARTOGRAPHY

COMPASS

DEAD RECKONING

EAST

ELEVATION

EQUATOR

GLOBE

LATITUDE

LONGITUDE

MAP

MERIDIAN

NORTH

RELIEF

SCALE

SEA LEVEL

SOUTH

SURVEY

TOPOGRAPHY

WEST

```
F N D E A D R E C K O N I N G Y S
W A A Q B Q D H H J W M G S E L N
J I H T R O N H T E S D V G A N O
U D J E L J P S H A P Q R Z X O I
E I V K I A E Q U O W M I O Z I T
A R Y D V W S S E Z Q M K O M T C
S E H K F I C W R P U N X H F A E
T M P X F L A T I T U D E Y K V R
E X A P J G L J H Z N G L O B E I
W M R G Q B E O D F H Q Z D O L D
V B G X P L C F N V O D Y I U E L
H S O U T H X O X G R V W P I F A
M O T T U V D B M S I C R J F C N
A P R O T A U Q E P F T X H E U I
P T A V W Q B A Y L A X U K I E D
V B C A V S L S C T O S Z D L W R
F K U A A E H D M T R S U E J A
C S U R V E Y R A D N U O B R N C
I A X E H Y B A T H Y M E T R Y B
N D L T X Y H P A R G O P O T I P
```

# WORD LADDER

Change just one letter on each line to
go from the top word to the bottom word.
Do not change the order of the letters.
You must have a common English word at each step.

BAG

_____

_____

JET

# SPIN THE DIALS

Imagine that each of the dials below can spin. Turn
each dial to form a 6-letter word reading straight
across the middle of the 3 dials.

*Answers on page 230.*

# MAZE-L TOV!

That's what we'll say if you can find
your way out of this one!

# GEO FIND IT

This is a word search with a twist. Instead of a list of words to find, we've given you a list of categories. Your challenge is to find 3 items in each category within the box of letters. Words can be found in a straight line horizontally, vertically, or diagonally. They may read either forward or backward.

3 African capitals

1. _____

2. _____

3. _____

3 countries with P names

1. _____

2. _____

3. _____

3 Baltic states

1. _____

2. _____

3. _____

3 European capitals

1. _____

2. _____

3. _____

3 islands

1. _____

2. _____

3. _____

```
E  L  K  I  N  S  H  A  S  A  V  G  V  W  T
V  G  A  R  P  A  B  R  U  S  S  E  L  S  W
V  T  B  G  U  I  R  H  P  R  J  O  Q  R  L
N  T  A  G  Y  V  Z  A  C  U  I  E  K  N  M
A  M  B  M  K  T  M  L  V  M  T  P  X  L  D
T  R  A  C  S  A  G  A  D  A  M  Z  O  N  I
S  Y  S  D  P  L  A  G  Z  L  J  H  A  P  J
I  C  I  V  M  A  L  I  S  D  K  L  M  W  I
K  G  D  V  M  M  I  Z  B  C  O  R  S  G  R
A  J  D  V  E  I  K  N  O  P  C  A  A  Y  I
P  Y  A  V  P  E  P  T  O  U  J  B  K  Q  C
E  T  Y  U  E  Y  S  H  W  T  U  I  R  L  D
K  I  B  O  R  I  A  N  P  C  S  R  Z  U  X
L  I  T  H  U  A  N  I  A  D  Y  E  K  A  C
L  Q  R  L  Q  F  O  E  K  F  M  T  M  H  C
```

# CODE-DOKU

Solve this puzzle just as you would a sudoku puzzle. Use deductive logic to complete the grid so that each row, column, and 3 by 3 box contains the letters from the word TRAVELING.

| | L | | | | | | V | |
| --- | --- | --- | --- | --- | --- | --- | --- | --- |
| | | | E | L | | | | G |
| | V | I | | | | E | T | |
| | N | G | | | R | T | | |
| | | | A | | I | | | |
| | | V | L | | | N | A | |
| | G | N | | | | A | I | |
| E | | | I | R | | | | |
| | A | | | | | E | | |

*Answers on page 231.*

# GOING IN CIRCLES

Find your way through these crazy circles!

*Answer on page 231.*

# GEOGRAPHY RIDDLES

Complete the crossword puzzle by filling
in the answer that fits each clue.

**ACROSS**

1. Morning times: abbr.
4. Omelet ingredient
7. America's "Uncle"
10. Haul a wrecked car
11. Zodiac lion
12. Stretch out, or stretch the truth
13. This number divided by itself equals itself
14. A U.S. state that fits this setup:
    ___ ___ O R ___ ___ A
16. Very angry
17. Biblical garden place
18. Hockey surface
19. Cannon sound
22. The "I" in this U.S. state separates two words that are opposites of each other
27. Has a meal
28. "Just _____ thought!"
29. U.S. state with a panhandle: abbr.
32. Tennis match part
33. U.S. state that fits this setup:
    ___ ___ O R ___ ___ A
37. Woman's name, or abbr. of Boise's state
38. Streets: abbr.

39. Raggedy girl doll
40. Catholic sister
41. Suffix for fast, high, and strong
42. Cloud's place
43. Photo _____ (White House events)

**DOWN**

1. Kind of clock, number, or energy
2. Where Monte Carlo is
3. Where Stockholm is
4. North Pole helper
5. Hair-styling stuff
6. Sticky stuff
7. Dove into a base
8. White House helper
9. Nasty
15. "Do _____ fa sol …"
19. "Who Wants to _____ Millionaire"
20. Halloween's month: abbr.
21. NFL "fifth quarters": abbr.
23. Far's opposite
24. Gambling house
25. Entirely gone, like car fuel
26. Tennessee's NFL team
29. Shrek, for example
30. Classic sneakers

31. Didn't win
34. Car fuel
35. Pen filler
36. "… have you _____ wool?"

| 1 | 2 | 3 | | 4 | 5 | 6 | | 7 | 8 | 9 |
|---|---|---|---|---|---|---|---|---|---|---|
| 10 | | | | 11 | | | | 12 | | |
| 13 | | | | 14 | | 15 | | | | |
| 16 | | | | | | 17 | | | | |
| 18 | | | | 19 | 20 | 21 | | | | |
| 22 | | | 23 | | | | | 24 | 25 | 26 |
| | | | 27 | | | | | 28 | | |
| 29 | 30 | 31 | | | | | | 32 | | |
| 33 | | | | 34 | 35 | 36 | | 37 | | |
| 38 | | | | 39 | | | | 40 | | |
| 41 | | | | 42 | | | | 43 | | |

# UNUSUAL PLACES

Every place name listed is contained within the group of letters. Names can be found in a straight line horizontally, vertically, or diagonally. They may read either forward or backward.

BENEVOLENCE (Georgia)

BIRD-IN-HAND (Pennsylvania)

BREAD LOAF (Vermont)

BUMBLE BEE (Arizona)

CHURCH (Iowa)

CUT AND SHOOT (Texas)

ELBOW (Saskatchewan)

FLIN FLON (Manitoba)

HOT COFFEE (Mississippi)

HYGIENE (Colorado)

LIZARD LICK (North Carolina)

MONKEYS EYEBROW (Kentucky)

OATMEAL (Texas)

ORDINARY (Virginia)

PAINT LICK (Kentucky)

PECULIAR (Missouri)

SANTA CLAUS (Indiana)

SPIDER (Kentucky)

SUCCESS (Missouri)

TOAST (North Carolina)

VIXEN (Louisiana)

WATERPROOF (Louisiana)

YUM YUM (Tennessee)

```
T  R  E  D  I  P  S  L  I  Z  A  R  D  L  I  C  K
B  S  P  H  D  F  Y  R  A  N  I  D  R  O  G  F  B
G  O  A  C  A  K  C  I  L  T  N  I  A  P  W  T  M
H  D  M  O  N  K  E  Y  S  E  Y  E  B  R  O  W  C
H  K  E  D  T  X  M  S  A  N  T  A  C  L  A  U  S
E  Y  Y  C  B  R  E  A  D  L  O  A  F  R  T  W  H
W  L  U  V  N  P  S  S  E  C  C  U  S  A  D  O  E
A  B  G  M  N  E  I  T  A  W  S  H  N  T  T  M  E
T  F  I  F  Y  C  L  Z  I  D  C  D  P  C  G  N  B
E  L  S  R  J  U  T  O  W  O  S  H  O  I  E  E  E
R  I  A  R  D  L  M  T  V  H  M  F  U  I  V  O  L
P  N  H  B  F  I  Z  D  O  E  F  A  G  I  A  R  B
R  F  C  J  J  A  N  O  D  E  N  Y  X  T  Q  E  M
O  L  R  U  U  R  T  H  E  J  H  E  M  L  L  S  U
O  O  U  R  R  M  O  A  A  P  N  E  B  B  I  I  B
F  N  H  F  Z  Z  Q  V  Z  N  A  V  O  I  F  B  K
D  H  C  B  Q  Z  M  J  G  L  D  W  S  T  F  X  L
```

# MORE UNUSUAL PLACES

Every place name listed is contained within the group of letters. Names can be found in a straight line horizontally, vertically, or diagonally. They may read either forward or backward.

BORING (Maryland)

BUTTERMILK (Kansas)

CHEDDAR (South Carolina)

CHIPMUNK (New York)

CONVENT (Louisiana)

DEVIL'S SLIDE (Utah)

DING DONG (Texas)

ENERGY (Illinois)

FROGTOWN (Virginia)

GOOFY RIDGE (Illinois)

GRAY MULE (Texas)

JOE BATT'S ARM (Newfoundland)

MOSQUITOVILLE (Vermont)

NIRVANA (Michigan)

PIE (West Virginia)

PRAY (Montana)

SUCK-EGG HOLLOW (Tennessee)

TICKTOWN (Virginia)

TIGHTWAD (Missouri)

TOAD SUCK (Arkansas)

TURKEY FOOT (Florida)

WAHOO (Nebraska)

WHAT CHEER (Iowa)

WHY (Arizona)

```
J O E B A T T S A R M X G F A K Y
G Y G D Y D W B N I R V A N A Y N
R F D E V I L S S L I D E R K A W
A W I H Y T V D I N G D O N G R O
Y X R E Z E W R A D D E H C P P T
M I Y S N L O X G T H D V F V E G
U N F E W L L Q Q C A P O D I N O
L T O H N I L X T W V L L P L C R
E T O K X V O M T I C K T O W N F
B N G X W O H H I J Y T P X X U C
S E I H L T G W M T O A D S U C K
E V Y U P I G N I R O B W A H O O
N N X I T U E B U T T E R M I L K
E O E C M Q K C H I P M U N K O S
R C R Z B S C T U R K E Y F O O T
G N R G K O U X A Y U S K X G A Q
Y A E E I M S W H A T C H E E R O
```

# A-MAZE-ING RACE

Can you get from Alaska to Zanzibar?
Actually, we'll settle for A to Z.

*Answer on page 231.*

# GETTIN' JIGGY

Quick—say the colors of the three words,
not the words!

RED  BLACK  YELLOW

# CROSSED WORDS

Unscramble the words in each line to solve the puzzle.
The words cross on a letter that they share.

*Clue: Family vacation getaway*

```
                          A
 O  O  O  T  S  D    R  U
                          T
                          G
                          E
```

# U.S. LANDMARKS

**ACROSS**

1. Monument Valley monuments
6. Havasu and Multnomah, e.g.
11. Actor in a crowd scene
12. "Have ___" (waiting room words)
13. Acadia National Park phenomenon
15. Bird of Arabian myth
16. Harangues
17. Black-and-white whale
19. "Messenger" molecule
20. High, rocky hills
22. Looped handle on a vase
25. Soda-can opener
27. Like a wrung dishcloth
29. Vast kingdoms
33. "Can ___ honest with you?"
34. Seattle landmark
36. Baseball great Combs
37. ___ off the old block
38. Crater, Superior, and others
39. Chaco Culture relics, e.g.

**DOWN**

1. Paris subway
2. Urge strongly
3. Siding plaster
4. "Prince Valiant" son
5. Former Iranian president Bani-___
6. Cereal usually served hot
7. Oregon Shakespeare Festival locale
8. July–August people
9. In ___ land (loopy)
10. "Let it stand," to an editor
14. Musician's asset
18. Magazine piece
21. Wraps for ranees
23. Greeted informally
24. Company cofounded by Spielberg
26. Newspaper editor Bradlee
28. Chicks' chirps
29. Düsseldorf donkey
30. Movie ratings org.
31. Central or Prospect
32. Blacken beef
35. French coin of old

|   |   |   |   |   |   |   |   |   |   |
|---|---|---|---|---|---|---|---|---|---|
| ¹ | ² | ³ | ⁴ | ⁵ | | ⁶ | ⁷ | ⁸ | ⁹ |
| ¹¹ | | | | | | ¹² | | | |

# ABOUT TURN

There's nowhere to go but up in this maze,
although you will make plenty of
left and right turns in the process.

*Answer on page 232.*

# PRETTY FONTSY!

Our favorite new inventor, Larry Letterman, has just been inspired by his name to create an alphabet soup using different fonts for the letters. He gave this presentation to a big soup company, but in a careless moment he put one letter in twice, in the same color, font, and size. He hates to repeat himself.
Can you find the letter?

*m*  **r**  h  **X**  t  *σ*  d  e  **G**  w  L  *ρ*  c  B
**H**  J  f  i  *N*  **Q**  *m*  *a*  ?  n  o  z  *  *V*
e  **L**  o  !  s  *k*  u  *f*  F  *y*  %  **+**  @  *g*
N  z  **D**  p  *W*  ?  x  **&**  a  T  *u*  **X**  *S*  c
*y*  b  H  *v*  R  k  q  I  c  j  E  t  p  *U*

# ISLANDS

Complete the word search to reveal a hidden word related to the puzzle's topic. Every word listed is contained within the group of letters. Words can be found in a straight line horizontally, vertically, or diagonally. They may read either forward or backward. Once you find all the words, you can read the hidden word from the remaining letters, top to bottom, left to right.

| | |
|---|---|
| ALAND | MALTA |
| ALCATRAZ | MAN |
| BALI | OKI |
| CORSICA | ORKNEY |
| CRETE | SAMOA |
| GALÁPAGOS | SARDINIA |
| HAINAN | SICILY |
| HONG KONG | SKYE |
| LONG | TAIWAN |
| LUZON | YAP |

LEFTOVER LETTERS: _____

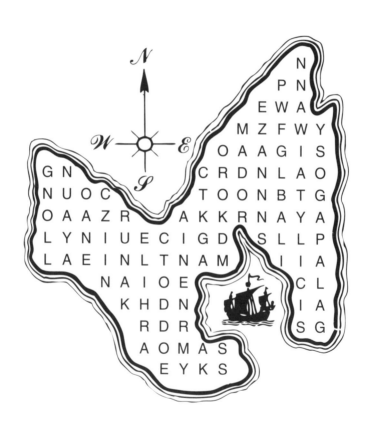

# CITY FIND IT

This is a word search with a twist. Instead of a list of words to find, we've given you a list of categories. Your challenge is to find 3 city names in each category within the box of letters. Names can be found in a straight line horizontally, vertically, or diagonally. They may read either forward or backward.

3 cities in Europe

1. _____

2. _____

3. _____

3 cities in Asia

1. _____

2. _____

3. _____

3 cities in North America

1. _____

2. _____

3. _____

3 cities in Russia

1. _____

2. _____

3. _____

B K O K I F I R O Q L M I D Z
H T O R O N T O I V U X H L M
M Z H L B T C C I A D K C T E
S B Y I E Q Y U U P B S O L X
T V M U G T U B B K F M S W I
P E T O Z N I E P I A T U E C
E F B Z S I L R S H T J G M O
T Y O T Q C U L E E C Q F J C
E S S N O B O D M Q S I L J I
R R T M B D E W Q R P W N P T
S B O G S W S W R G Q M Q U Y
B F N N P R E W T N A R W M M
U J L H Q L C D Z D S H U K E
R C S V B A R C E L O N A U J
G Y F R C H O N T G A C J V R

# SPIRAL DESIGN

Both statues below (A and B) contain spiral designs.
Statue B is a mirror image of A yet something is wrong.
Can you spot the difference between the 2 statues?

A.

B.

Answer on page 233.

Which piece of cheese (A, B, or C)
is cut from the semicircle below?

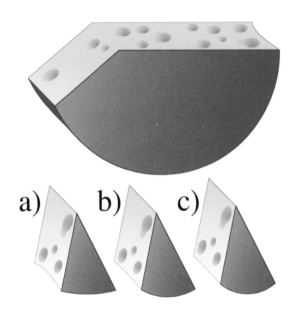

a)     b)     c)

# AMERICA A TO Z

Every word in this alphabetical list is contained within the group of letters. Words can be found in a straight line horizontally, vertically, or diagonally. They may read either forward or backward.

| | |
|---|---|
| AMERICA | NATION |
| BEAUTIFUL | OFFICE |
| CONSTITUTION | PRESIDENT |
| DEMOCRAT | QUEST |
| ELECT | REPUBLIC |
| FOUNDING | SENATE |
| GOVERNMENT | TERRITORY |
| HOUSE | UNION |
| INDEPENDENT | VEEP |
| JUSTICE | WASHINGTON |
| KENTUCKY | X-MAS |
| LEGISLATE | YELLOWSTONE |
| MILITARY | ZOO |

```
S  Q  I  F  X  Y  K  C  U  T  N  E  K  G  D  J  P
V  Y  M  J  N  B  E  A  U  T  I  F  U  L  V  J  V
N  Z  D  Y  J  F  M  N  I  Z  R  L  N  S  A  M  X
C  N  K  L  Y  E  E  T  A  L  S  I  G  E  L  L  J
G  O  V  E  R  N  M  E  N  T  G  S  V  X  O  C  Q
U  O  B  I  E  O  C  A  B  T  C  E  L  E  J  K  D
U  V  C  J  U  S  T  I  C  E  E  N  Q  P  Z  N  N
E  A  E  F  B  I  N  D  E  P  E  N  D  E  N  T  D
S  C  N  X  O  N  O  I  T  U  T  I  T  S  N  O  C
U  I  O  N  A  D  U  V  R  P  D  G  H  K  R  W  D
O  L  T  P  S  E  N  A  T  E  E  W  J  F  M  Q  G
H  B  S  H  N  K  V  R  F  L  S  L  Y  O  I  P  B
Y  U  W  K  C  W  C  D  D  W  W  K  P  U  L  L  G
Y  P  O  F  P  T  X  N  K  H  X  X  U  N  I  O  N
N  E  L  P  R  E  S  I  D  E  N  T  Q  D  T  E  K
R  R  L  G  L  I  Y  J  B  O  K  Z  U  I  A  C  Q
C  T  E  R  R  I  T  O  R  Y  L  M  E  N  R  I  N
Z  Q  Y  A  A  Y  V  X  M  D  Y  N  S  G  Y  F  G
C  O  I  T  A  R  C  O  M  E  D  R  T  D  A  F  S
X  N  O  T  G  N  I  H  S  A  W  Z  T  U  G  O  N
```

# WORLDLY FOOD

Every food listed is contained within the group of letters. Words can be found in a straight line horizontally, vertically, or diagonally. They may read either forward or backward. The leftover letters spell out an additional fact.

BLOOD PUDDING

BORSCHT

CAVIAR

CHITLINS

CROCODILE STEAKS

CURRY

ESCARGOT

GEFILTE FISH

GRASSHOPPER TACOS

GRITS

HAGGIS

LUTEFISK

MISO

OWL SOUP

SASHIMI

SOUSE

SPOTTED DICK

SYLTA

TRIPE

VEGEMITE

WITCHITY GRUB

LEFTOVER LETTERS: _____

```
            I  S  I  G  G  A  H
         G  N  A  P  U  O  S  L  W  O  D
      D  E  I  R  O  T  I  O  O  C  N  T  O
      C  R  F  A  K  T  E  S  C  A  R  G  O  T  G
      O  C  I  O  S  T  D  I  A  L  O  E  W  N  A
   U  S  V  L  T  I  E  Y  R  T  A  C  L  I  I  C  T
   A  A  N  T  M  F  D  R  S  R  E  O  D  T  E  H  H
   C  A  T  E  S  E  D  R  M  E  S  D  O  C  K  I  C
   E  D  G  F  E  T  I  U  M  P  U  I  U  H  M  T  S
   O  E  E  I  S  U  C  C  T  P  O  L  R  I  I  L  R
   V  C  P  S  H  L  K  B  D  O  S  E  H  T  U  I  O
   R  G  I  H  E  R  S  O  C  H  A  S  M  Y  M  N  B
      A  R  E  L  S  O  C  U  S  A  T  R  G  I  S
      R  T  Y  A  L  T  N  D  S  C  E  O  R  S  O
         K  L  B  E  D  I  K  A  A  A  N  U  O
            G  Y  A  R  O  R  R  O  K  M  B
               S  E  A  T  G  S  S
```

# ITALY

Every word listed is contained within the group of letters. Words can be found in a straight line horizontally, vertically, or diagonally. They may read either forward or backward. The leftover letters spell out an additional fact.

| | |
|---|---|
| ANTIPASTO | PARMESAN |
| ARMANI | PASTA |
| COLOSSEUM | PISA |
| DANTE | PIZZA |
| ESPRESSO | POPE |
| FIAT | RISOTTO |
| FLORENCE | ROME |
| GENOA | SICILY |
| MACHIAVELLI | TINTORETTO |
| MICHELANGELO | TUSCANY |
| MILAN | VENICE |
| NAPLES | VERDI |

LEFTOVER LETTERS: _____

```
                    N M P I
                T A L U A A I Y I E
            S   O N E S S L F Z T
        Y L I C I S T I E O I N Z
        F T O T S A P I T N A M H A
        E F L O R E N C E D T
    G I L L E V A I H C A M
        R O T T E R O T N I T
        C E A       T I L C A D
            E           N S E T S R E
                        R O G I E E S
                        G O T N N M V
                          E F T A A R
                          N A O L M A
                            O S S E R P S E E
                            A R N H A T P
                                A C O R Y A
                                N P I O N D F A
                                  L M A     S H
                                    E C
                                    C S I
                                    I U O
                                    N T
                                    E N
                                    V
```

# CITY SITES

Can you match these famous sites in the left column
to their respective cities in the right column?

| | |
|---|---|
| LA SCALA | NEW ORLEANS |
| TAJ MAHAL | LONDON |
| BASIN STREET | BEIJING |
| LEFT BANK | TOKYO |
| COLOSSEUM | PARIS |
| PICCADILLY CIRCUS | HAVANA |
| KREMLIN | MILAN |
| FORBIDDEN CITY | AGRA |
| GINZA | ROME |
| MORO CASTLE | MOSCOW |

*Answers on page 234.*

How many times does the letter F
appear in this sentence?

*Answer on page 235.*

# EUROPEAN CAPITALS

Every word or phrase listed is an anagram (rearrangement) of a European capital. First, unscramble the letters to figure out the name, then search for it in the grid. Names can be found in a straight line horizontally, vertically, or diagonally. They may read either forward or backward.

| | |
|---|---|
| BEACH RUTS | LIKE SHIN |
| BIN REL | MORE |
| BUN LID | NON-OLD |
| CHANGE OPEN | OAF IS |
| DID RAM | RAW SAW |
| DUB TAPES | RED BAGEL |
| EZ GRAB | RUBS LESS |
| GEAR UP | SLOB IN |
| HAS NET | SMART DAME |
| I SPAR | SOLO |
| IN NAVE | TALL INN |
| JERKY KIVA | TEAL VAT |

```
R E Y K J A V I K D M A O S P G P
Y P O T S E P A D U B E G Q P N Z
F B R U S S E L S B E T T D O D R
W A R S A W Z J V L V C P B Y S H
C N S J G K G M H I S V S O F I A
B R E X A X W K F N T I G I U M M
B E W G B E R G A Z L S P Q J M S
I D L B A R P J V L S X H F Y T T
K Y H G L H G Q O V Y I Q P G S E
N P T N R B N N C M A D R I D E R
I R A K G A D E V B C F X A L R D
S X L L N O D A P P N L W V P A A
L O L Z N J L E R O R O M E R H M
E S I S T E X A Z F C M T N M C P
H L N A T E G B E R L I N V X U E
T O N T F U A T H E N S S W B B A
L S A G E P A A N N E I V X S A G
```

# MOSAIC MAZE

Don't let the squares confuse you. You can mosey from start to finish in a flash. Take the fastest route.

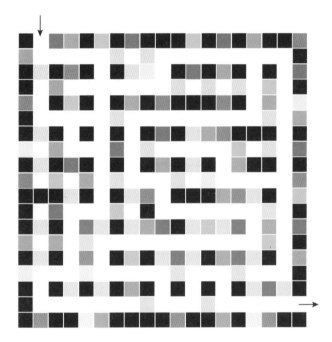

*Answer on page 235.*

# WORD LADDER

Use the clues to change just one letter on each line to go from the top word to the bottom word. Do not change the order of the letters. You must have a common English word at each step.

TRUCK

_____ or treat

_____ a pain in the neck

_____ sound of typed keys

_____ oily smoothness

_____ lazing about on the job

SNACK

# SIX CITIES TO SEE

**ACROSS**

1. Capital on the Nile
6. Czech capital
12. Bit of mischief
13. French epic hero
14. Blockage fixer
15. "My sentiments exactly"
16. Literally, "lion city"
18. Lang. that gave us "dachshund"
19. Major leagues, slangily, with "the"
23. Dugong or manatee
27. Hang decoratively
28. Early Peruvian
29. Tar
30. Daisy supporter
31. Align the crosshairs
32. Largest metropolis on the Mediterranean
38. One with a crush
41. Kidney-related
42. Tribeca Film Festival cofounder
43. Like a noble gas
44. Gorky Park locale
45. 32nd Olympiad host

**DOWN**

1. "Mama" ___ Elliot
2. Dead against
3. Calif.-to-Fla. highway
4. Engagement gift
5. Stop sign shape
6. Earlier conviction, on a rap sheet
7. Jungle bellow
8. High-school math
9. Fish with a long snout
10. French one
11. Palindromic Dutch city
17. Bench for the faithful
20. "Sam ___" from "Green Eggs and Ham"
21. 4.0 is a great one
22. Capitol Hill VIP
23. Bro's twin, perhaps
24. MD concerned with tonsils
25. Top fighter pilot
26. Plain cotton fabric
27. Point off, as for bad behavior
29. [quoted verbatim]
31. Quiver unit
33. Prefix with sol or space
34. Comedian Jay
35. Short race distance, briefly
36. Old-timey "not"
37. Between soprano and tenor
38. Farragut's rank: abbr.
39. "In excelsis ___" (holiday lyric)
40. Slip-___ (mules, e.g.)

# TOTALLY CUBULAR!

As if he weren't diabolical enough, legend has it that the inventor of this cube has a dark side. Not content to produce a puzzle that can be solved only by bright 8-year-olds, his evil twin came up with a maze on top of a cube. Would you kindly come to the rescue of the black dot in the top colored square and help it get to the gray square at the bottom-right corner?

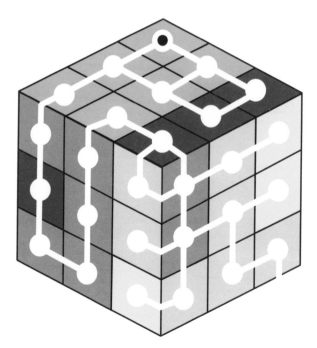

*Answer on page 236.*

# LOST CITY MAZE

Follow the path to the lost city.

*Answer on page 236.*

# COUNTRIES AND CAPITALS

Every South American country and capital city listed is contained within the group of letters. Names can be found in a straight line horizontally, vertically, or diagonally. They may read either forward or backward.

*Bonus: Can you match each country with its capital?*

ARGENTINA

ASUNCIÓN

BOGOTÁ

BOLIVIA

BRASÍLIA

BRAZIL

BUENOS AIRES

CARACAS

CHILE

COLOMBIA

ECUADOR

GEORGETOWN

GUYANA

LIMA

MONTEVIDEO

PARAGUAY

PARAMARIBO

PERU

QUITO

SANTIAGO

SUCRE

SURINAME

URUGUAY

VENEZUELA

BONUS: _____

```
C  U  J  C  M  A  S  A  R  G  E  N  T  I  N  A  C
O  R  B  E  H  M  M  P  O  E  C  U  A  D  O  R  Y
M  E  V  S  I  I  C  U  N  U  U  B  R  A  Z  I  L
O  P  Z  A  L  K  L  T  W  B  R  A  S  I  L  I  A
N  P  E  N  E  Q  I  E  O  I  U  L  B  P  Z  A  A
T  I  B  T  W  T  F  E  T  O  G  J  U  R  B  T  O
E  R  V  I  I  C  K  A  E  L  U  S  E  Z  J  O  B
V  A  E  A  N  A  Y  U  G  A  A  U  N  N  M  G  I
I  S  N  G  M  O  G  X  R  C  Y  R  O  Z  P  O  R
D  U  E  O  D  C  T  Q  O  V  F  I  S  B  N  B  A
E  N  Z  K  K  D  X  G  E  C  C  N  A  F  Y  S  M
O  C  U  U  L  H  R  O  G  A  N  A  I  V  B  M  A
B  I  E  O  F  W  I  A  R  K  X  M  R  O  S  K  R
V  O  L  Y  A  U  G  A  R  A  P  E  E  T  U  M  A
P  N  A  E  M  M  C  W  S  X  J  E  S  I  C  S  P
N  E  R  I  U  A  I  B  M  O  L  O  C  U  R  B  M
H  R  O  V  S  Q  A  I  V  I  L  O  B  Q  E  I  C
```

# TOURIST ATTRACTIONS

Oops! A new worker at the USA visitors center removed three-letter words from 12 major tourist attractions. Each missing word was rounded up and put into the box below. Can you put each word into an empty space to name the real attractions?

ACE  BET  CAT  COT

ELL  HIT  IRE  LIB

OLD  RAN  TOW  USE

1. __ __ __ S Y   R O S S
   H O U S E (Philadelphia)

2. A L __ __ __ R A Z
   I S L A N D (San Francisco)

3. E M P __ __ __   S T A T E
   B U I L D I N G
   (New York City)

4. E P __ __ __
   C E N T E R (Orlando)

5. F __ __ __ K L I N
   I N S T I T U T E
   (Philadelphia)

6. G E T T Y   M __ __ __ U M
   (Los Angeles)

7. G __ __ __ E N   G A T E
   B R I D G E (San Francisco)

8. L I B E R T Y
   B __ __ __ (Philadelphia)

9. W I L L I S
   __ __ __ E R (Chicago)

10. S P __ __ __
    N E E D L E (Seattle)

11. S T A T U E   O F
    __ __ __ E R T Y
    (New York City)

12. W __ __ __ E   H O U S E
    (Washington, D.C.)

Answers on page 237.

# CHECKERBOARD PUZZLE

Moving diagonally, can you find a single, unbroken path from the circle in the upper left corner to the diamond in the lower right? Your path must alternate between circles and diamonds. There's only one way to do it.

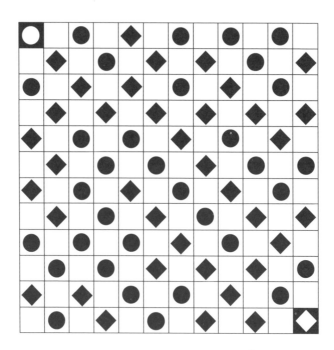

# AROUND THE WORLD

Every place name in this alphabetical list is contained within the group of letters. Place names can be found in a straight line horizontally, vertically, or diagonally. They may read either forward or backward.

| | |
|---|---|
| AUCKLAND | NIGERIA |
| BORDEAUX | ORLANDO |
| CYPRUS | PORT-AU-PRINCE |
| DALLAS | QUEBEC |
| EAST TIMOR | RIGA |
| FIJI | SLOVENIA |
| GHENT | TEHRAN |
| HELSINKI | UNITED KINGDOM |
| IRELAND | VENICE |
| JUBA | WASHINGTON |
| KIEV | XALAPA |
| LUXEMBOURG | YUCATÁN |
| MOLDOVA | ZANZIBAR |

```
U   N   I   T   E   D   K   I   N   G   D   O   M   G   M   N   N
V   E   I   K   E   A   S   T   T   I   M   O   R   O   T   N   A
G   C   A   H   A   Z   T   X   S   Q   Q   Z   C   O   U   S   R
Y   V   G   K   K   R   C   O   L   T   U   A   K   X   V   K   H
P   H   I   T   N   E   H   G   O   B   E   N   P   E   O   H   E
P   E   R   M   T   X   E   Z   V   O   B   Z   N   R   D   C   T
E   G   S   O   G   A   C   U   E   R   E   I   M   F   I   J   I
A   N   V   L   S   L   N   A   N   D   C   B   D   U   Q   L   H
I   O   I   D   V   A   I   I   I   E   T   A   J   P   G   Y   P
R   T   K   O   B   P   R   R   A   A   O   R   L   A   N   D   O
E   G   N   V   S   A   P   E   A   U   R   Z   I   Q   G   G   J
G   N   I   A   D   S   U   L   U   X   E   M   B   O   U   R   G
I   I   S   X   A   I   A   A   U   B   J   Q   K   T   F   D   B
N   H   L   J   L   P   T   N   A   Q   U   K   Y   Z   T   M   O
Y   S   E   X   L   B   R   D   N   P   B   C   Y   P   R   U   S
Y   A   H   H   A   D   O   N   A   T   A   C   U   Y   W   Z   P
O   W   V   W   S   C   P   L   A   U   C   K   L   A   N   D   B
```

# ROAD WORK

This puzzle follows the rules of your typical word search: Every word listed is contained within the group of letters. Words can be found in a straight line horizontally, vertically, or diagonally. They may read either forward or backward. But, in this version, words wrap up, down, and around the 3 sides of the cube.

| | |
|---|---|
| ALLEY | DRIVE |
| AVENUE | HIGHWAY |
| BOULEVARD | INTERSTATE |
| BRIDGE | LANE |
| BYPASS | MEWS |
| BYWAY | PARKWAY |
| CIRCLE | ROAD |
| CLOVERLEAF | STREET |
| COURT | TERRACE |
| CRESCENT | THOROUGHFARE |
| CUL-DE-SAC | THRUWAY |
| DEAD END | TUNNEL |
| DETOUR | TURNPIKE |

*Answers on page 237.*

**113**

# WORD LADDER

Change just one letter on each line to go from the top word to the bottom word. Do not change the order of the letters. You must have a common English word at each step.

CAMP

_____

_____

_____

SITE

# OHIO ANAGRAM

What 3 words, formed by different arrangements of the same 6 letters, can be used to complete the sentence below?

The joyriders _____ around _____, Ohio, and watched as stores were _____ during the riot.

Answers on page 237.

# SEE YOUR WAY FREE

You seem to have somehow wandered into a
kaleidoscope. Now you need to find your way out
before someone shakes it and you get all pixilated.

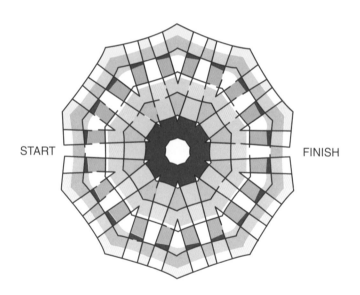

START

FINISH

*Answer on page 238.*

# THE STATE OF THINGS

Every state listed is contained within the group of letters. States can be found in a straight line horizontally, vertically, or diagonally. They may read either forward or backward.

| | |
|---|---|
| ALABAMA | MAINE |
| ALASKA | MICHIGAN |
| ARIZONA | MISSISSIPPI |
| COLORADO | MISSOURI |
| CONNECTICUT | MONTANA |
| DELAWARE | NEVADA |
| FLORIDA | NEW YORK |
| GEORGIA | OHIO |
| HAWAII | OREGON |
| IDAHO | TEXAS |
| ILLINOIS | UTAH |
| INDIANA | VERMONT |
| KANSAS | VIRGINIA |
| KENTUCKY | WYOMING |
| LOUISIANA | |

```
F O T O S S C K A A S R H Y I H
A G I U A I R O N L M A K A E V
I H E X C O O A L I A C S N T E
O N E O Y I I N S O U B I N L U
E T D W R S T S I T R A A A A R
N E E I I G I C N L M A D M M K
I N N U A S I E E G L I D O A W
H A O V S N K A N N R I N O T E
A L M I I N A I D U N T V E R S
T L P I O R M F O E A O V A A T
H P A G C O G S L N L E C R E A
I A E S Y H S I A O R A I I D O
A R W W K I I M N M R Z W A H T
O O B A M A E G O I O I V A C O
N T E N I T P N A N A E D H R I
L I P P I I T A A N N I N A S E
```

# HOLD YOUR TONGUE!

Every language listed is contained within the group of letters. Words can be found in a straight line horizontally, vertically, or diagonally. They may read either forward or backward. The leftover letters spell out a riddle and its answer.

ARABIC

BENGALI

BURMESE

CHINESE

DUTCH

ENGLISH

FRENCH

GERMAN

HINDI

ITALIAN

JAPANESE

JAVANESE

KOREAN

PERSIAN

POLISH

PORTUGUESE

PUNJABI

ROMANIAN

RUSSIAN

SPANISH

THAI

TURKISH

UKRAINIAN

VIETNAMESE

LEFTOVER LETTERS: _____

```
T H E H H I F U Y P S E
T H A I S L R K P U E A S A
K E N I A E R V N E R E E R
Y D L G N A S J S A L V U A
I O N C I N A E B N I G G E
P E H N A B N I N E U A U S
B G I M I A C T T I E I T E
N A R R P N H N U A H T R M
N E H A O H A S N R L C O R
G N J E W M C I I A K I P U
O G R L E D A T S N E I A B
W L H S A T A N U R A R S N
R I E E T H E Y I D E P O H
E S C E S E N A V A J P S K
H H O R U S S I A N E S
```

# CHOPPER LINES

Which line is longer, red or blue?

*Answer on page 238.*

# WORD LADDER

Use the clues to change just one letter on each line to go from the top word to the bottom word. Do not change the order of the letters. You must have a common English word at each step.

HANG

_____ it's connected to your arm

_____ when a plane reaches its destination

_____ part of the road

_____ you wait in it, sometimes

_____ a tart fruit

TIME

# ASIAN ANAGRAMS

Every word or phrase listed is an anagram (rearrangement) of an Asian country or territory. First, unscramble the letters to figure out the name, then search for it in the grid. Names can be found in a straight line horizontally, vertically, or diagonally. They may read either forward or backward.

| | |
|---|---|
| A COMA BID | MAT VINE |
| ALSO | NAIL ARKS |
| AM I NEAR? | NOISE IN AD |
| BAN HUT | OH TAKE OURS |
| BE RUIN | PAGE IRONS |
| BLADE HANGS | PASTA KIN |
| CHAIN | PENAL |
| ERRANT HOOK | RAIN |
| GAIN LOOM | RAM MANY |
| I WANT A… | SAIL A YAM |
| IN AID | SERIAL |
| LAD IN HAT | SHIP LIP PINE |

```
Z N O E P Y E Z W M R S K Z E F S G C
L A H A J D N A L I A H T O A U B N P
S W G I R K S M T J I F O F H T P X P
G I I S I V G N P Q S I N G A P O R E
X A E E Y E Z O Q G T F T U P A F U K
I T M N D I L A E R O K H T U O S A T
L M D O N A I L O G N O M L F Z K Z P
L A T D E A A K I R P Q T V Q N I H A
B L I N P M O H F B Q I W L A L B N K
Z A Y I E R S E N I P P I L I H P A I
N Y N R A M N A Y M R F I L N T K R S
O S V G N O R T H K O R E A E N D I T
M I G Z L N E P A L S E A I M I F C A
A A Q W M A I M C H I N A W R C V B N
N S P A F W D S Q O N G S D A W L H I
T D L K O X F E I E N U R B U W I U H
E Q A Z A X V O S R A F G E U L K T F
I Q O I S R A E L H C A M B O D I A K
V F S H A M Q V L W A T N V Y O S N F
```

# SOUTH AMERICA SCRAMBLE

Every word or phrase listed is an anagram (rear-rangement) having to do with South America. First, unscramble the letters to figure out the word, then search for it in the grid. Words can be found in a straight line horizontally, vertically, or diagonally. They may read either forward or backward.

A COMB OIL

A HICCUP CHUM

CAN I?

DO A CURE

FEARS INTRO

FLAB TOOL

INFESTED A ROOT

MR. ZERO AVIAN

PLAZA

RENT AGAIN

ROADIE JOINER

SASH PIN

SEDAN

TOUPEE RUGS

VIA BOIL

ZEAL VENUE

```
A U K X L B U B B O L I V I A W D
R R J X M P O R T U G U E S E U E
G C O L O M B I A K V X T X P H F
E J S Q S B X V R L S C E O Z C O
N C F Q W G N H V Y A U E A I C R
T H S I N A P S N M Q W L Q N I E
I B N F O O T B A L L E R Y Z P S
N F F A S R X Z H M U V C C I U T
A U C R C K O K I Z U F W O H H A
D O R I E N A J E D O I R D T C T
H S I L R Z I N E C U A D O R A I
X K E I D H E H L Z A P R H N M O
T S V D T V L D T A L A P A Z E N
J E D Z N O C B P P G R R V O T V
R R M J W A Y C Q P X Z C S I U Y
R D A I V P I W J D K J L R Z X L
Y R A I N F O R E S T C Y Y W Y B
```

# AFRICAN ADVENTURE

**ACROSS**

1. Come out of one's shell?
6. Barely perceptible
11. Buffett's hometown
12. "Let's call it ___" ("We're even")
13. African peak visible from some safaris
15. The Tar Heels of the NCAA
16. Librarian's deg.
17. Many a PX customer
18. Rapper who co-starred in "The Italian Job"
20. Many a safari sighting
21. Blundered
23. Serengeti grazer that may be seen on safari
26. Island with colossal carved heads
30. "Riddle-me-___" ("Guess!")
31. Commercials, briefly
32. Realm that lasted roughly one thousand years: abbr.
33. Safari fare
36. Desk tray labels
37. Spanish epic hero
38. Contract provisions
39. Works on fall leaves

**DOWN**

1. Malarkey
2. ___ acid (protein builder)
3. Baby powders
4. Tai ___ (exercise method)
5. Toolbox item
6. Indoor coolers
7. Word that modifies a noun (abbr.)
8. Tehran native
9. Drug cop, for short
10. Runners at the corners, say, in baseball
14. School in upstate NY named for a "great" Saxon king
19. Michael C. Hall title character, for short
20. Mormon Church inits.
22. Less challenging
23. Comet's path
24. Get together, as grads
25. "Answer ___ no, please"
27. Like molasses
28. Bert's Muppet pal
29. Clarinet parts
31. "Hamlet" has five
34. Run smoothly, as an engine
35. 1970s kidnapping grp.

|     |     |     |     |     |     |     |     |     |     |
|-----|-----|-----|-----|-----|-----|-----|-----|-----|-----|
| ¹   | ²   | ³   | ⁴   | ⁵   |     | ⁶   | ⁷   | ⁸   | ⁹   | ¹⁰  |
| ¹¹  |     |     |     |     |     | ¹²  |     |     |     |     |
| ¹³  |     |     |     |     | ¹⁴  |     |     |     |     |     |
| ¹⁵  |     |     |     | ¹⁶  |     |     |     | ¹⁷  |     |     |
| ¹⁸  |     |     | ¹⁹  |     |     |     | ²⁰  |     |     |     |
|     |     |     | ²¹  |     |     | ²²  |     |     |     |     |
| ²³  | ²⁴  | ²⁵  |     |     | ²⁶  |     |     | ²⁷  | ²⁸  | ²⁹  |
| ³⁰  |     |     |     | ³¹  |     |     |     | ³²  |     |     |
| ³³  |     |     | ³⁴  |     |     |     | ³⁵  |     |     |     |
| ³⁶  |     |     |     |     |     | ³⁷  |     |     |     |     |
| ³⁸  |     |     |     |     |     | ³⁹  |     |     |     |     |

Answers on page 240.

# TYPES OF MAPS

Every word listed is contained within the group of letters. Words can be found in a straight line horizontally, vertically, or diagonally. They may read either forward or backward.

ATLAS

CARTOGRAM

CLIMACTIC

GLOBE

NAUTICAL

GEOLOGICAL

PHYSICAL

POLITICAL

RELIEF

STREET

THEMATIC

TIME ZONE

TOPOGRAPHIC

WEATHER

L A C I T U A N K M L P N
P R C I H P A R G O P O T
O S N Q T I M E Z O N E T
L P T H K A O R E L I E F
I T K R I Q M J Q H V U M
T T B N E G O E L H T U A
I Y E R D E Y A H R S N R
C Y X J F O T V H T H N G
A M L A C I G O L O E G O
L A C I S Y H P I T Z L T
E M G B K A T L A S D O R
V Q C L I M A C T I C B A
K T Z S W E A T H E R E C

# ROLL THE DICE

Study the dice—which red dot is bigger?

*Answer on page 240.*

# UNITED STATES GEOGRAPHIC TRIVIA

How well do you know your geography?
Check your skills with these questions.

1. There is only one place in the United States where four states meet at a single point. Where is it?

2. Which state (or states) borders on the most other states? How many states does it (or do they) border?

3. Heading west, could you exit West Virginia and enter Maryland?

4. Which state is farther north: Colorado or Wyoming?

5. Which state borders only one other U.S. state?

*Answers on page 240.*

# AFRICAN ANAGRAMS

Every word or phrase listed is an anagram (rearrangement) of an African country. First, unscramble the letters to figure out the name, then search for it in the grid. Names can be found in a straight line horizontally, vertically, or diagonally. They may read either forward or backward.

| | |
|---|---|
| A GUN AD | MAIL |
| A HANG | MASCARA GAD |
| AND US | NO GALA |
| ARIA AIM NUT | ON BAG |
| ARUBA OF SKIN | PATIO HIE |
| BE INN | REIGN |
| CARE MOON | RELEASE IRON |
| CARVE DEEP | SEEN GAL? |
| DUB RUIN | SLY LEECHES |
| GO TO | SWAN BOAT |
| I BIT JUDO | TEARIER |
| IN A SUIT | UNIQUE ALGAE RATIO |
| LAW AIM | WARN AD |

```
I  Z  C  A  P  E  V  E  R  D  E  M  F  I  G  A  B  O  N
A  R  A  A  E  N  I  U  G  L  A  I  R  O  T  A  U  Q  E
I  U  I  L  M  F  M  G  N  B  H  N  X  S  N  O  Y  Y  W
S  B  N  B  W  H  A  A  S  U  K  N  I  E  O  Q  G  T  D
I  O  A  M  S  N  D  N  C  R  O  Q  L  N  R  M  G  O  V
N  T  T  X  A  U  A  D  W  K  C  X  T  E  E  S  G  I  T
U  S  I  A  S  L  G  A  J  I  O  D  W  G  G  B  W  U  A
T  W  R  E  I  X  A  O  O  N  I  Z  P  A  I  T  W  R  N
S  A  U  R  E  M  S  W  S  A  T  U  O  L  N  G  P  B  G
E  N  A  T  R  E  C  D  I  F  U  I  D  N  U  R  U  B  O
Y  A  M  I  R  H  A  W  R  A  O  J  N  Z  T  N  D  O  L
C  I  Q  R  A  W  R  A  W  S  B  H  C  D  A  O  Y  Z  A
H  L  L  E  L  D  A  Z  W  O  I  X  L  R  C  O  V  A  I
E  X  D  W  E  S  M  N  M  Z  J  S  B  A  R  R  D  L  G
L  X  N  Q  O  D  N  A  D  K  D  Q  Z  G  G  E  A  K  N
L  Q  C  P  N  F  X  X  Y  A  B  F  S  L  H  M  L  Q  Q
E  R  L  W  E  D  A  A  E  T  H  I  O  P  I  A  R  V  B
S  B  O  D  W  S  F  W  P  Q  Z  X  E  D  F  C  N  W  Z
A  U  J  J  O  E  W  O  E  Q  F  C  Q  A  K  H  X  A  B
```

# U.S. TRIVIA

See if you can answer these trivia questions about the names of U.S. states.

1. Other than the three states that begin and end with the letter A (Alabama, Arizona, and Alaska), what other state (or states) begin and end with the same letter?

2. Florida begins with two consonants. Does any other state? If so, what state(s)?

3. In which states can you find Carol, Diana, Ida, and Mary?

4. What letter (or letters) is not found in the name of any state?

5. Every other letter in the name of one state is the same. Which state is it?

Answers on page 241.

# GOT HOT

Each clue leads to a 2-word answer that rhymes, such as BIG PIG or STABLE TABLE. The numbers in parentheses after the clue give the number of letters in each word. For example, "cookware taken from the oven (3, 3)" would be "hot pot."

1. Became overheated (3, 3): _____

2. Rudely ignore baby bear (3, 4): _____

3. Sluggish river current (4, 4): _____

4. College housing application (4, 4): _____

5. More elegant cruise ship (5, 5): _____

6. Earthquake cause (4, 5): _____

7. Reading room with tracked-in muck (5, 5): _____

8. Arrive at sandy expanse (5, 5): _____

9. Unpleasant surprise from a market decline (5, 5):

   _____

10. Majestic raptor (5, 5): _____

# TRAVELING IN STYLE

You won't have to go far to find these glamorous autos. Every word listed is contained within the group of letters. Words can be found in a straight line horizontally, vertically, or diagonally. They may read either forward or backward.

| | |
|---|---|
| ACURA | LAMBORGHINI |
| ALFA ROMEO | LAND ROVER |
| ASTON MARTIN | LEXUS |
| AUDI | LINCOLN |
| BENTLEY | LOTUS |
| BMW | MASERATI |
| BUGATTI | MERCEDES-BENZ |
| CADILLAC | PORSCHE |
| FERRARI | ROLLS-ROYCE |
| INFINITI | SAAB |
| JAGUAR | VOLVO |

```
Q A I N L O C N I L I B C C B
D L T E A M Q T A D U E B A Q
P A X U M U H V U K B N S L U
K U F O B U G A T T I T D L Y
S V W J O U J X J V O L S I H
A M Z M R A R G N N Q E A D A
B K X O G X M U M F A Y N A E
T F S U H M F A S Y O P M C M
H I A L I A R I S E N F Y I T
V R K F N T B N M E F O M I S
Z A P E I R O O R P R Z S T F
B R D N B L R S L S U A D I H
Y R E K O A L E L E A B T N J
O E Y V F S B L H B A O L I B
D F L L O Z O B O C L G B F J
A O A M E R C E D E S B E N Z
V C Q U U F D A D N F R K I V
O B U V S X O N G D W T O G O
A S Z R S B Y Y A Q E B G P K
J C V I A S U T O L R G Z I L
```

# LEAST POPULOUS PLACES

Every place listed is contained within the group of letters. Place names can be found in a straight line horizontally, vertically, or diagonally. They may read either forward or backward.

| | |
|---|---|
| ANTARCTICA | MONGOLIA |
| AUSTRALIA | NAMIBIA |
| BOTSWANA | NAURU |
| CHRISTMAS ISLAND | NIUE |
| COCOS ISLANDS | PALAU |
| COOK ISLANDS | PITCAIRN ISLANDS |
| DOMINICA | SABA |
| FALKLAND ISLANDS | SAN MARINO |
| FRENCH GUIANA | SIBERIA |
| GIBRALTAR | SURINAME |
| GREENLAND | TOKELAU |
| ICELAND | TUVALU |
| LIECHTENSTEIN | VATICAN CITY |
| MONACO | WESTERN SAHARA |

```
A  N  A  W  S  T  O  B  D  B  E  Z  S  H  F  A  E
L  S  D  N  A  L  S  I  S  O  C  O  C  P  A  C  U
A  A  I  R  E  B  I  S  L  G  E  C  P  I  L  I  I
I  G  I  B  R  A  L  T  A  R  A  A  K  T  K  T  N
L  S  T  U  V  A  L  U  C  T  N  N  S  C  L  C  W
A  I  B  I  M  A  N  J  H  L  A  O  A  A  A  R  U
R  D  N  A  L  N  E  E  R  G  I  M  N  I  N  A  E
T  I  L  A  L  H  G  W  I  Y  U  R  I  R  D  T  M
S  M  R  I  Y  U  D  E  S  T  G  Z  E  N  I  N  A
U  E  C  L  W  A  A  S  T  I  H  D  T  I  S  A  N
A  J  D  O  A  L  C  T  M  C  C  N  S  S  L  N  I
G  O  X  G  O  E  I  E  A  N  N  A  N  L  A  O  R
T  H  A  N  T  K  N  R  S  A  E  L  E  A  N  F  U
U  N  X  O  X  O  I  N  I  C  R  E  T  N  D  A  S
D  R  O  M  I  T  M  S  S  I  F  C  H  D  S  A  Y
W  V  U  Q  P  T  O  A  L  T  M  I  C  S  B  D  U
J  Y  R  A  W  B  D  H  A  A  G  O  E  A  H  G  R
N  A  L  C  N  O  V  A  N  V  N  B  I  P  X  J  J
N  A  C  A  S  P  D  R  D  B  T  D  L  C  R  I  R
U  K  S  S  A  N  M  A  R  I  N  O  S  N  Q  A  H
```

# FIVE INTERNATIONAL CITIES

## ACROSS
1. Costume-ball coverings
6. Hong Kong neighbor
11. Have ___ with: talk to
12. In any way
13. Petronas Twin Towers city
15. Airport schedule abbr.
16. "The Fresh Prince of ___-Air"
17. Beatles label
18. Middleman's transaction
20. Richie's Mom, to the Fonz
21. City visited by pilgrims
23. Halloween symbols
26. Sarcastic laugh
30. Command level: abbr.
31. Word before diem or capita
32. Gold, to Guatemalans
33. Capital of Argentina
36. Belted constellation
37. Have a bite of
38. Eiffel Tower city
39. Daggers of old

## DOWN
1. Manufacturer
2. Less than 90 degrees, as an angle
3. Herring varieties
4. Carrier to Seoul
5. Groom's place
6. Really rough up
7. Bank machine, for short
8. Bank heist, e.g.
9. College reunion attendees
10. First saint canonized by a pope
14. "Attack of the Giant ___" (1959)
19. Early times, briefly
20. Damage slightly
22. Diamond measures
23. Dizzy Gillespie's music
24. Honda's luxury line
25. Churchill's "___ Finest Hour"
27. Bronco or mustang
28. Alpine ridge
29. Kentucky Derby winner's garland
31. Lily of operatic fame
34. "There's ___ in team"
35. Actor McShane of "Deadwood"

|  1 |  2 |  3 |  4 |  5 |    |  6 |  7 |  8 |  9 | 10 |
|----|----|----|----|----|----|----|----|----|----|----|
| 11 |    |    |    |    |    | 12 |    |    |    |    |
| 13 |    |    |    |    | 14 |    |    |    |    |    |
| 15 |    |    |    | 16 |    |    |    | 17 |    |    |
| 18 |    |    | 19 |    |    |    | 20 |    |    |    |
|    |    |    | 21 |    |    | 22 |    |    |    |    |
| 23 | 24 | 25 |    |    | 26 |    |    | 27 | 28 | 29 |
| 30 |    |    |    | 31 |    |    |    | 32 |    |    |
| 33 |    |    | 34 |    |    |    | 35 |    |    |    |
| 36 |    |    |    |    |    | 37 |    |    |    |    |
| 38 |    |    |    |    |    | 39 |    |    |    |    |

# CIRCLE TAKES THE SQUARE

All you have to do to solve this puzzle is move in a single, unbroken path from the circle in the upper left corner to the circle in the lower right. Your path must alternate between circles and squares, and you can only move horizontally and vertically (not diagonally). There's only one way to do it.

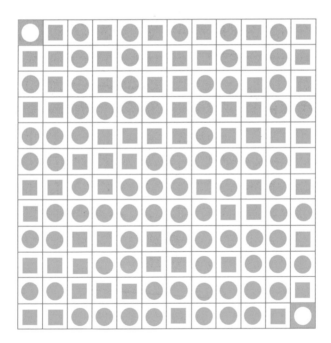

*Answer on page 242.*

# TOTALLY CUBE-ULAR!

Which of the shapes below can be folded to form the cube in the center? There may be more than one.

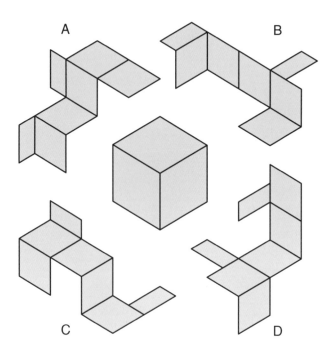

A

B

C

D

# THE BAHAMAS

Every word or phrase listed is contained within the group of letters. Words can be found in a straight line horizontally, vertically, or diagonally. They may read either forward or backward. Leftover letters will reveal a fact about the island country.

ABACO

ACKLINS

ANDROS ISLAND

ARCHIPELAGO

BASKETRY

BIMINI

BOATING

COMMONWEALTH

CRAB FEST

ELEUTHERA

EXUMA

FISHING

GREAT INAGUA

HANDICRAFTS

LONG ISLAND

MAYAGUANA

NASSAU

NEW PROVIDENCE

REGATTAS

SAILING

SCUBA DIVING

SWIMMING

TOURISM

LEFTOVER LETTERS: _____

```
N T H E O G A L E P I H C R A
B E L E U T H E R A T A H G U
S S W I M M I N G L A M A N G
S A I P E X U M A N M T C I A
L U T H R L B E D E A S T V N
W O T T A O W H O U Y E G I I
U A S S A N V S T A A F N D T
N D B T O G D I C O G B I A A
A Y I M A I E I D S U A H B E
A N M N C S D R C E A R S U R
G O I S K L E V E R N C I C G
C N N H L A O C A B A C F S U
S A I L I N G N D R E F E D M
I S L A N D N B A S K E T R Y
D N A L S I S O R D N A D S S
```

# WORD LADDER

Use the clues to change just one letter on each line to go from the top word to the bottom word. Do not change the order of the letters. You must have a common English word at each step.

SEEK

_____ flowers grow from this

_____ what you click after writing an email

_____ repair

_____ you may occasionally change it

FIND

*Answers on page 243.*

# SPACE RACE

Help the astronaut land on the moon by navigating his spaceship through the solar system.

# IN SWITZERLAND

## ACROSS

1. Swiss peaks
5. Beyond the norm
10. Fifth-century pope called "the Great"
11. The New Yorker caricaturist Edward
12. View from Lausanne
14. Racing champion Tom
15. "Oh, sure!"
16. Greek goddess of dawn
18. Before, in sonnets
19. Having no seacoast, like Switzerland
23. Ending for Brooklyn
24. Entrepreneur-helping gp.
25. Thomas Hardy's "___ of the d'Urbervilles"
27. Moral standard
31. Noted Swiss peak
33. "Forgive ___ trespasses…"
34. Bible's "hairy man"
35. Kosovo minority
36. Apartment dweller's payment

## DOWN

1. Know-it-___ (cocky types)
2. Jack Sprat's choice
3. Jab with one finger
4. Filtered, as flour
5. Employ for a purpose
6. Anderson of sitcoms
7. "Jeopardy!" host
8. Admire greatly
9. Having wings
13. British prisons
17. Like a judge, in a saying
19. Acid-testing paper
20. Opposite of "Attention!"
21. "Iliad" wise man
22. Author of "My Antonia"
26. Ticket part you keep
28. Garden waterer
29. Where to find Tehran
30. King of early Britain: var.
32. Trauma ctrs.

|   |   |   |   |   |   |   |   |   |
|---|---|---|---|---|---|---|---|---|
| ¹ | ² | ³ | ⁴ |   | ⁵ | ⁶ | ⁷ | ⁸ | ⁹ |

# STATE BIRDS

Every state bird listed is contained within the group
of letters. Birds can be found in a straight line
horizontally, vertically, or diagonally. They may
read either forward or backward.

GREAT ROADRUNNER
(NM)

HERMIT THRUSH (VT)

LARK BUNTING (CO)

MOCKINGBIRD (AR, FL,
MS, TN, TX)

MOUNTAIN BLUEBIRD
(ID, NV)

MOURNING DOVE (WI)

NENE (HI)

NORTHERN CARDINAL
(IL, IN, KY, NC, OH, WV,
VA)

NORTHERN FLICKER (AL)

PEREGRINE FALCON (ID)

PURPLE FINCH (NH)

ROBIN REDBREAST (MI)

RUFFED GROUSE (PA)

WESTERN MEADOWLARK
(KS, MT, ND, OR, WY)

WILD TURKEY (MA,
OK, SC)

WILLOW GOLDFINCH
(WA)

WILLOW PTARMIGAN
(AK)

WOOD DUCK (MS)

```
N M O U N T A I N B L U E B I R D
O C U R U F F E D G R O U S E P I
C K P M O C K I N G B I R D F T I
L Q U A S I O T O B X U F B E G F
A G R E A T R O A D R U N N E R P
F N P H P B N W Z D C P Z I J J I
E I L R O B I N R E D B R E A S T
N T E E M O U R N I N G D O V E Z
I N F I N W I L D T U R K E Y O V
R U I R H E R M I T T H R U S H O
G B N C K L N T Z F R E E U P I V
E K C U D D O O W E N H J K C W D
R R H C N I F D L O G W O L L I W
E A W I L L O W P T A R M I G A N
P L N O R T H E R N F L I C K E R
N O R T H E R N C A R D I N A L N
W E S T E R N M E A D O W L A R K
```

*Answers on page 243.*

# UP AND OVER

Starting at the top left, navigate your way through this up-and-over maze. Prepare for plenty of zigs and zags!

*Answer on page 244.*

# 90 DEGREES

How many 90-degree angles are hidden in this image?

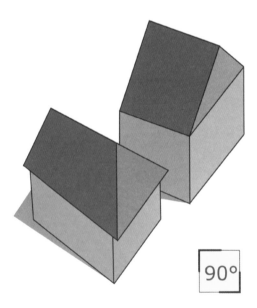

90°

# BRAZIL

Every term associated with Brazil listed is contained within the group of letters. Words can be found in a straight line horizontally, vertically, or diagonally. They may read either forward or backward. The leftover letters spell out an additional fact about Brazil.

AMAZON

ANTEATER

BOSSA NOVA

BRASÍLIA

CARNIVAL

IGUAÇU FALLS

JAGUAR

MACAW

MOUNTAINS

OCELOT

OPOSSUM

ORINOCO RIVER

PARDO

PARROTS

PLAINS

PORTUGUESE

PUMA

RAIN FOREST

RIO DE JANEIRO

SAMBA

SÃO PAULO

SLOTH

SOUTH AMERICA

WILDLIFE

LEFTOVER LETTERS: _____

```
T H O R I E N A J E D O I R E
S P O P O S S U M E C T A A C
C U L L A P O R T U G U E S E
R A P A R R O T S M G A M L N
N C R I E U A B L A H T O L S
F I R N V E S R J C T B U A I
V R E S I A L A O A F O N F C
A E T R R V P S N W S S T U I
A M A Z O N A I I V A S A C A
O A E L C I R L S O M A I A O
C H T N O E D I P O B N N U F
E T N T N L O A P H A O S G E
L U A G I R U E U A T V E I S
O O T F R L S H M O W A S O N
T S E R O F N I A R E A R T H
```

# VACATION DESTINATIONS

Every word listed is contained within the group of letters. Words can be found in a straight line horizontally, vertically, or diagonally. They may read either forward or backward.

ATLANTIC CITY

BERMUDA

BUSCH GARDENS

CAMPING TRIP

CARIBBEAN

CHINA

CLUB MED

COAST

CRUISE

DENALI

DISNEY WORLD

ECO TOUR

EUROPE

FLORIDA KEYS

HAWAII

HOLLYWOOD

LAKE COTTAGE

LAS VEGAS

MEDITERRANEAN

MOUNTAIN CABIN

NATIONAL PARK

NEW YORK CITY

NIAGARA FALLS

RAIN FOREST

SEASIDE

SEA WORLD

SHORE

SKI LODGE

VIRGIN ISLANDS

WORLD TOUR

```
D L R O W A E S S E A S I D E
I L A N E D G L A S V E G A S
R S J J E E D T T I P C E A G
X U D I K M O B G U E N T O K
N Y O N B B L D D R H L N R N
A I L T A U I Q O C A V A D S
E R B A O L K H V N I P E O N
B U E A K C S F T T L I N O E
B O R T C E E I W A I Q A W D
I T M O L N C C N A Q S R Y R
R D U T P C I O W I O M R L A
A L D S I E I A T O G A E L G
C R A T S H S T T I R T O H
R O Y N A D E T N N A N I H C
A W V N Q P A D F S U G D V S
D I S N E Y W O R L D O E P U
S L L A F A R A G A I N M M B
Q W H K N E W Y O R K C I T Y
T A B Z S Y E K A D I R O L F
P I R T G N I P M A C A N N R
```

# MAZE

Find your way through the tangled maze.

*Answer on page 245.*

# RHYME TIME

Each clue leads to a 2-word answer that rhymes, such as BIG PIG or STABLE TABLE. The numbers in parentheses after the clue give the number of letters in each word. For example, "cookware taken from the oven (3, 3)" would be "hot pot."

1.  Equal portion (4, 5): _____

2.  Hip place to go to class (4, 6): _____

3.  Zoom by (5, 4): _____

4.  Tidy high schooler (5, 4): _____

5.  Light bite for a group of wolves (4, 5): _____

6.  Seat with no rounded edges (6, 5): _____

7.  Young cow's chuckles (5, 6): _____

8.  Nicer restaurant (5, 5): _____

9.  Crazy chocolate (4, 5): _____

10. One who cuts the grass with less haste (6, 5):

   _____

11. Took black chunks from a mine (5, 4): _____

*Answers on page 245.*          **159**

# ROAD TRIP

Every word listed is contained within the group
of letters. Words can be found in a straight line
horizontally, vertically, or diagonally. They may
read either forward or backward.

| | |
|---|---|
| AUTOMOBILE | MAP |
| BRIDGE | MOTEL |
| CAMPING | OVERLOOK |
| DINER | ROAD SIGNS |
| EXIT RAMP | ROUTE |
| FAST FOOD | SEAT BELT |
| GAS STATION | SIGHTSEEING |
| HOTEL | SLUG-A-BUG |
| INTERSTATE | SNACKS |
| I SPY | SPEED LIMIT |
| ITINERARY | TOLLWAY |
| LICENSE PLATES | TUNNEL |
| LUGGAGE | TWENTY QUESTIONS |

```
N  L  I  C  E  N  S  E  P  L  A  T  E  S  E  L  O
B  O  H  Q  E  L  K  T  O  L  L  W  A  Y  E  D  C
P  J  I  T  S  Z  C  I  H  P  R  I  G  T  O  Y  T
M  L  U  T  E  Z  A  N  B  I  D  N  O  I  K  O  W
A  O  G  A  A  G  N  T  D  L  I  M  L  M  O  G  E
R  R  U  U  T  T  S  E  Z  E  N  L  U  I  O  Q  N
T  O  B  T  B  B  S  R  E  A  E  V  G  L  L  V  T
I  A  A  O  E  Y  S  S  Y  U  R  S  G  D  R  W  Y
X  D  G  M  L  C  T  T  A  F  J  I  A  E  E  T  Q
E  S  U  O  T  H  C  A  A  G  B  Q  G  E  V  U  U
D  I  L  B  G  M  P  T  J  K  Y  R  E  P  O  N  E
G  G  S  I  T  I  N  E  R  A  R  Y  I  S  U  N  S
F  N  S  L  X  C  A  M  P  I  N  G  L  D  R  E  T
F  S  L  E  T  O  H  W  A  S  C  O  N  V  G  L  I
Y  Z  Z  N  Q  U  X  M  G  P  E  C  R  J  H  E  O
N  O  X  L  Q  J  A  M  A  Y  V  P  M  A  Q  T  N
D  O  O  F  T  S  A  F  Q  P  N  G  V  R  P  U  S
```

# CITY NICKNAMES

Every city nickname listed is contained within the group of letters. Nicknames can be found in a straight line horizontally, vertically, or diagonally. They may read either forward or backward.

ANCHORTOWN
(Anchorage, AK)

CHARM CITY (Baltimore, MD)

CHI-TOWN (Chicago, IL)

CINCY (Cincinnati, OH)

CITY OF ROSES
(Pasadena, CA)

CITY OF TREES
(Sacramento, CA)

COW CHIP CAPITAL
(Beaver, OK)

CRABTOWN (Annapolis, MD)

DOGTOWN
(Santa Monica, CA)

THE EMPIRE CITY
(New York City, NY)

FOG CITY (San Francisco, CA)

HANGTOWN (Placerville, CA)

HOTLANTA (Atlanta, GA)

IRON CITY (Pittsburgh, PA)

JET CITY (Seattle, WA)

LA-LA-LAND
(Los Angeles, CA)

MOTOR CITY (Detroit, MI)

NOLA (New Orleans, LA)

THE OLD PUEBLO
(Tucson, AZ)

PALMETTO CITY
(Charleston, SC)

ROCKET CITY
(Huntsville, AL)

SPACE CITY (Houston, TX)

SPAMTOWN, USA
  (Austin, MN)
THE STEEL CITY (Gary, IN)
SURF CITY, USA
  (Huntington Beach, CA)

VALLEY OF THE SUN
  (Phoenix, AZ)
VICE CITY (Miami, FL)

```
T H E E M P I R E C I T Y Y C N I C L
T L I K O P A L M E T T O C I T Y V I
R O C V T I A S U Y T I C F R U S A V
U L H Y O X I E Q Z V C Y Q O C P E E
A B A T R K V W R X A V T E Q I A N E
P E R I C O O G N I L U I R P L M M N
M U M C I I C Y U L L G C L H A T C A
P P C T T R R Y Y N E J E Q Y T O I A
L D I E Y O A N W J Y R C T T I W T N
W L T K T N B O W V O T I U I P N Y W
T O Y C T C T M U O F C V C C A U O O
F E M O X I O Z A C T J Y C L C S F T
O H D R H T W B P E H G I T E P A R R
G T N C Z Y N A J H E M O O E I C O O
C I T Y O F T R E E S H J D T H V S H
I A N W O T G N A H U N C W S C M E C
T A D O K J H M U P N C T K E W G S N
Y B C H L A L A L A N D J H H O Q E A
Y C L S P A C E C I T Y L M T C D Z G
```

In each balloon is the name of a country, minus one letter. Find the missing letters that complete each name, and write it on the blank line. Then rearrange those missing letters to spell another country.

1. _____     4. _____     7. _____

2. _____     5. _____     8. _____

3. _____     6. _____     9. _____

Bonus country: _____

1.

2.

3.

4.

5.

6.

7.

8.

9.

**164**

*Answers on page 245.*

# GEOGRAPHY SCRAMBLEGRAM

Four 11-letter words, all of which revolve around the same theme, have been jumbled. Unscramble each word, and write the answer in the accompanying space. Next, transfer the letters in the shaded boxes into the shaded keyword space, and unscramble the 9-letter word that goes with the theme. The theme for this puzzle is geography.

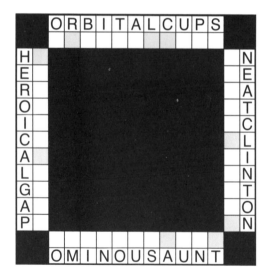

ORBITALCUPS

HEROICALGAP

NEATCLINTON

OMINOUSAUNT

# CARD GAMES

Get shuffling to find every card game listed within the group of letters. Words can be found in a straight line horizontally, vertically, or diagonally. They may read either forward or backward.

ALL FOURS

AUTHORS

BACCARAT

BEGGAR-MY-NEIGHBOR

BEZIQUE

BLACKJACK

BRIDGE

CANASTA

CANFIELD

CRIBBAGE

ÉCARTÉ

EUCHRE

FAN-TAN

GIN RUMMY

GO FISH

HEARTS

KLONDIKE

NAPOLEON

NEWMARKET

OLD MAID

PIQUET

POKER

PUT AND TAKE

QUADRILLE

ROUGE ET NOIR

RUSSIAN BANK

SEVEN-CARD STUD

SNIP SNAP SNORUM

THREE CARD BRAG

WHIST

```
P T T S X S M D G S N R Z I K
O C H H T I C N O E L O P A N
K K R R R H C Y F V O D H N A
E E A I O E S H I E L O E W B
R E B M B T E L S N D W A M N
H O U R H B O C H C M M L U A
C R U Q G S A Z A A A D L R I
U V E G I G D G R R I X F O S
E Z K D E Z U K E D D N O N S
Y G I L N E E K Y S A B U S U
K I D E Y T T B E T W G R P R
A N N I M B U N N U W H S A L
S R O F R H L A O D U G I N G
P U L N A B F A E I S H F S A
Y M K A G B A C C A R A T P T
Y M X C G Y A B S K V B I I S
T Y I C E C A R T E J Q L N A
W M N W B S R O H T U A W S N
X Q U A D R I L L E G F C J A
C E K A T D N A T U P R W K C
```

# WORD LADDER

Use the clues to change just one letter on each line to go from the top word to the bottom word. Do not change the order of the letters. You must have a common English word at each step.

PLANE

______

______ a braid

______

______ an inflammation

______

TRAIN



*Answers on page 246.*

# SQUARE HOLDINGS

Which of the 2 interior squares are exactly the same?

# CROSS COUNTRY

Can you help this vacationing family make it from southern California all the way to Maine?

*Answer on page 246.*

# DIAGONAL JUMP

Can you find a single unbroken path from the circle
in the upper left corner to the circle in the lower right?
Your path must move from circle to circle, with one
twist—you can jump over any one diamond, as
long as there is a circle on the opposite side of it.
There's only one way to do it.

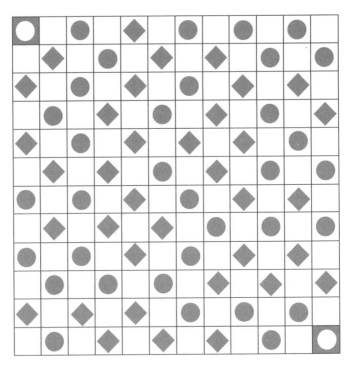

# AFRICAN CAPITALS

Every capital listed is contained within the group of letters. Names can be found in a straight line horizontally, vertically, or diagonally. They may read either forward or backward.

| | |
|---|---|
| ABIDJAN | KINSHASA |
| ABUJA | LILONGWE |
| ACCRA | LOME |
| ALGIERS | LUSAKA |
| BAMAKO | MALABO |
| BANGUI | MAPUTO |
| BANJUL | MASERU |
| BISSAU | MOGADISHU |
| CAIRO | MONROVIA |
| CONAKRY | NAIROBI |
| DAKAR | NIAMEY |
| FREETOWN | NOUAKCHOTT |
| HARARE | PORT LOUIS |
| KAMPALA | PORTO NOVO |
| KIGALI | RABAT |

TRIPOLI                 YAOUNDE

TUNIS

```
        Q I Z F G
      N U K G I I Z    R M
    V G I E U H S I D A G O M
  M N G H A R P I N S K S J N
V A A L A P M A K E T A B A R I
B L N W O T E E R F E D H N H Z
I A B I S S A U Y A L G I E R S L
A B I D J A N T T O H C K A U O N S
  O H B A N J U L U P O R T L O U I S K
    F D F       U H M F C O R I A C N K B
                B M C K P I L Y V U X
                L A M Y P P O A Q T
                P O R T O N O V O
                U N K S L G U F N
                T R A L I W N W U
                O O N N B E D H
                N V O L O M E B
                Y I C U R Z A S
                H A Z S I M K
                  V J A A G
                  F C K N
                  D O A
```

Answers on page 246.          

# OLD NAMES

We've given you the old names (no longer in use) of cities and countries that have changed their names at some point. Your job is to figure out the current names, then search for those names in the grid.

1. EAST PAKISTAN

_ _ _ _ _ _ _ _ _ _

2. BRITISH HONDURAS

_ _ _ _ _ _

3. ABYSSINIA

_ _ _ _ _ _ _ _

4. GOLD COAST

_ _ _ _ _

5. SAINT-DOMINGUE

_ _ _ _ _

6. PERSIA

_ _ _ _

7. MESOPOTAMIA

_ _ _ _

8. CONSTANTINOPLE

_ _ _ _ _ _ _ _

9. EAST AFRICA PROTECTORATE

_ _ _ _ _

10. FRENCH SUDAN

_ _ _ _

11. BURMA

_ _ _ _ _ _

12. NEW AMSTERDAM

_ _ _ _ _ _ _ _ _ _ _

13. CEYLON

_ _ _ _ _ _ _ _

14. SIAM

_ _ _ _ _ _ _ _

15. SOUTHERN RHODESIA

_ _ _ _ _ _ _ _

```
K J O W I A K R A K R E S Z F
A M Z I P V A Y X X T B H H G
N S F D V R N L B H E R Q L L
E K K N C E B B I T C E Q U U
W P B H K S K O B H T W F P B
Y H O A A G P Y E A V B S S N
O N Y Z N I U W L I S A I S A
R V A C A G T F I L R B O R T
K Q A R I X L I Z A N M H I S
C K E J Z S I A E N Y I B L I
I S S B A L R J D D R Z M A A
T I M Y A N M A R E C R N N T
Y G R M Y H V Q E K S B A K E
D T V A C X E B M H K H K A I
L X T T N Q Y B R L G T P K Q
```

# ON THE MAP

## ACROSS

1. Old sailors
5. Christmas gifts, often
9. Hosp. trauma areas
12. Away from wind
13. Chew the scenery
15. Birds, in Latin
16. Land of lemurs and tomato frogs
18. Gusto
19. Curvy figure
20. Most eligible, once
21. Red lights and flares
23. Gets on one's nerves
24. Boat landing
25. Century plants and others
28. Some candy buys
32. Legendary birthplace of Apollo
33. Bonus country formed from the first letters of the four longest answers, clockwise from 16-Across
34. It has a code
35. "Love ___ leave…"
36. Certain chess piece, informally
37. Inclined type, for short
38. "___, old chap!"
39. Bar assoc. member
40. Toss from the game
41. Old phone call cost
43. Praises mightily
44. Ballpark figure words

45. "You Can't Get a Man with ___"
46. 1998 Olympics city in Japan
49. Certain MIT grad.
50. Michele of "Glee"
53. Boxers Muhammad and Laila
54. Country of 3 districts, 12 cantons, and 106 communes
57. Piece of the whole
58. "Faust," for one
59. Sudden hankering
60. Belt maker's tool
61. Go up and down the dial
62. Old Olds autos

## DOWN

1. Far from feral
2. Cry of dismay
3. Ruby and crimson
4. Honeydrippers' hit "___ of Love"
5. Gives props to
6. Caravan stopovers
7. "Village People" hit
8. "Apologia pro vita ___"
9. "When will they ___ learn?"
10. Take a coffee break
11. Concordes, briefly
14. Place for a "little house"
15. Country whose national animal is the Karabakh horse

17. Al and Tipper
22. Guitar great ___ Paul
23. World's leading producer of cocoa
24. ___ -walsy: friendly
25. Let in or let on
26. Canadian fliers
27. Take out ___ (borrow money)
28. Shopping meccas
29. Old Russian co-op
30. Respond to a stimulus
31. Old sailors
33. Inspirational slogan
36. Fictional pilot who said, "Never tell me the odds"

40. Bel Air, to Los Angeles
42. Coastal eagle
43. "I Am the Walrus" figure
45. "It's the end of ___"
46. Big wine valley
47. What there oughta be
48. Sadie Hawkins Day chaser
49. Corp. officer
50. Fisherman's enticer
51. Therefore, to Descartes
52. Def Leppard hit "Rock of ___"
55. Delivery company called "Brown"
56. "They're playing ___ song"

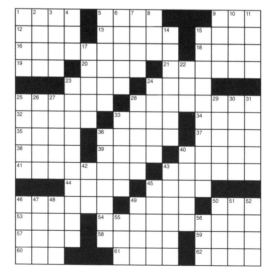

Answers on page 247.

# FRANCE

Every word listed is contained within the group of letters. Words can be found in a straight line horizontally, vertically, or diagonally. They may read either forward or backward. The leftover letters spell out an additional fact about France.

| | |
|---|---|
| ARC DE TRIOMPHE | LILLE |
| CARDIN | THE LOUVRE |
| CEZANNE | LYON |
| COCO CHANEL | MARSEILLE |
| DE GAULLE | MONA LISA |
| DEGAS | MONET |
| EIFFEL TOWER | NANTES |
| EURO | NAPOLEON |
| FASHION | NICE |
| FENCING | PARIS |
| FRANC | PICASSO MUSEUM |
| GENDARME | PYRENEES |
| GIVENCHY | RENOIR |
| GRAND PRIX | TOULOUSE |
| INTERPOL | WINE |

LEFTOVER LETTERS: _____

```
F R P I C A S S O M U S E U M A
N C L E N A H C O C O C E I S R
S G U A R C D E T R I O M P H E
O R M E C A R D I N O Y L A T W
O A I M E S R O E O A E F R E O
R N P Y H C N E V I G N R I E T
D D Y T D E G A S H O I T S F L
A P R S R T L T H S E W H E E E
X R E L L I E S R A M A N G S F
E I N O L N M F N F B C E U C F
N X E L O P R E T N I A O U S I
N E E M O A A M O N A L I S A E
A F S T N H D E G A U L L E E G
Z E O C M E N A P O L E O N T R
E R V U O L E H T I C S H A P E
C O F I T S G T E R R I T O R Y
```

# COPYRIGHTS

Are each pair of letters in these typographical symbols the same size, or are they different?

*Answer on page 247.*

# TRAFFIC TANGO

The 4 pedestrians at the bottom of the maze each need to get where they're going. Destination 1 is a store, 2 is a car, 3 is a home, and 4 is a bicycle. Use the visual clues to decide who is going where, and then guide each on his or her way. Their paths will cross, so don't let them end up in the wrong place!

# POPULAR ATTRACTIONS

Every attraction listed is contained within the group of letters. Words can be found in a straight line horizontally, vertically, or diagonally. They may read either forward or backward.

ACROPOLIS

ANGKOR WAT

BIG BEN

BLUE MOSQUE

BURJ KHALIFA

CHARLES BRIDGE

CHICHÉN ITZÁ

CN TOWER

COLOSSEUM

CRATER LAKE

EIFFEL TOWER

GATEWAY ARCH

GRAND CANYON

GREAT SPHINX

HAGIA SOPHIA

LIBERTY BELL

MACHU PICCHU

NATIONAL MALL

NIAGARA FALLS

OLD FAITHFUL

SPACE NEEDLE

STONEHENGE

TAJ MAHAL

TIMES SQUARE

TIVOLI GARDENS

VERSAILLES

VICTORIA FALLS

WHITE HOUSE

WINDSOR CASTLE

YELLOWSTONE

```
S T I V O L I G A R D E N S N R U A
I X E I F F E L T O W E R D A E Q I
L T I M E S S Q U A R E W C Q W T L
O E U M G G G R A N D C A N Y O N G
P R L A H A M J A T K Z X E J T L N
O L D F A I T H F U L H V S Q N T A
R X N I H P S T A E R G P Q V C Z T
C V U L J R G A T E W A Y A R C H I
A I M A C H U P I C C H U R N N M O
G C L H C I C H E N I T Z A U V N
N T T K L S T O N E H E N G E I E A
E O U J V L L E B Y T R E B I L R L
B R A R S T E K A L R E T A R C S M
G I N U B D Y C O L O S S E U M A A
I A G B L E N O T S W O L L E Y I L
B F K E S U O H E T I H W I O Y L L
K A O G S L L A F A R A G A I N L G
Z L R A I H P O S A I G A H O A E D
B L W I N D S O R C A S T L E F S B
W S A P S F U M B L U E M O S Q U E
Z N T C H A R L E S B R I D G E M A
```

# GEOGRAPHAGRAMS

The letters in each of the 12 words below can be rearranged to form the names of 12 countries. Is your geographic knowledge sharp enough to unscramble all 12?

1. ALSO _____

2. CHAIN _____

3. ENEMY _____

4. LAITY _____

5. MAIL _____

6. MOAN _____

7. PAINS _____

8. PLANE _____

9. PURE _____

10. RAIN _____

11. REGALIA _____

12. SERIAL _____

*Answers on page 248.*

# PYRAMID LINES

Are lines A and B the same length?

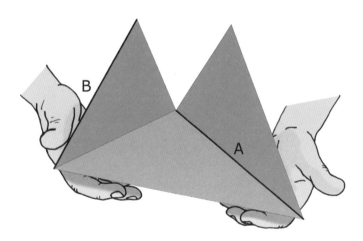

# STAR CONTRAST

Are the octagons within the Yin-Yang
symbol the same color?

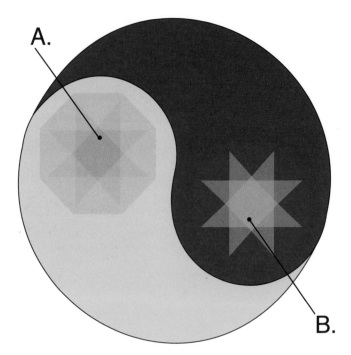

A.

B.

*Answer on page 248.*

# A CAPITAL PUZZLE!

Can you find a state capital hiding
in each sentence below?

1. "Here's the plan: Sing along with the karaoke
   and try not to embarrass yourself!"

2. Radioactive isotope? Ka-boom!

3. "Oh yes," said the florist, "I know that garden
   very well."

4. You can get good deals on the wholesale
   market.

5. Architect: "Send those gazebos to Newark."

# FLORIDA

Every word listed is contained within the group of letters. Words can be found in a straight line horizontally, vertically, or diagonally. They may read either forward or backward.

| | |
|---|---|
| BUSCH GARDENS | MIAMI |
| CLEARWATER | NAPLES |
| DAYTONA | ORANGES |
| DISNEY WORLD | ORLANDO |
| DOLPHINS | PALMS |
| EVERGLADES | PANTHERS |
| GATORS | PENSACOLA |
| HEAT | SARASOTA |
| JACKSONVILLE | SEMINOLES |
| KEYS | SOUTH BEACH |
| LAKELAND | ST. PETERSBURG |
| MAGIC | TALLAHASSEE |
| MARLINS | TAMPA |

```
H C A E B H T U O S   J A C K S O N V I L L E
K I T A L A K E L A N D I L P A L M S O O C
A G A T O S A R A S D I S N E Y W O R L D
P A E V E R G L A D E S L T N A P L E S N
R M H         D S M J R S Q R K M A A
              I A A H X W X Q L
              N C M P R A S R
              O O M O A P T O
              T L L L B R P E S
              Y A B E U D E T R
              A Q T M S O T A E
              D   A I C L E M H
                  L A H P R P T
              Q G L M G H S A N
              U A A I A I B T A
              J T H R R N U O P
                O A M D S R U K
                R S H E A G B
                S S W N A L U
                  E G S V E
              T A E H T Q
          D K E Y S
```

# EXOTIC TRAVEL

Every word listed is contained within the group of letters. Words can be found in a straight line horizontally, vertically, or diagonally. They may read either forward or backward.

| | |
|---|---|
| ANTIGUA | GUAM |
| BALI | HAWAII |
| BANGKOK | LONDON |
| BARCELONA | LOS ANGELES |
| BORA BORA | MADRID |
| CAIRNS | MALTA |
| CANNES | MANHATTAN |
| CAYMAN ISLANDS | MARBELLA |
| CHAMONIX | MELBOURNE |
| COSTA DEL SOL | MOROCCO |
| CROATIA | PARIS |
| CYPRUS | PRAGUE |
| DUBAI | RIO DE JANEIRO |
| DURBAN | ROME |
| FLORENCE | SYDNEY |
| GALÁPAGOS | VENICE |

```
B  J  Z  V  G  A  L  A  P  A  G  O  S  X  H
O  G  Z  U  S  O  S  R  N  I  R  D  E  I  M
M  I  A  C  N  I  A  M  R  I  N  C  L  T  A
V  M  L  D  R  G  U  I  E  A  S  F  E  U  R
M  A  O  A  U  O  C  N  L  W  B  O  G  A  B
G  N  P  E  B  S  A  S  E  A  K  I  N  B  E
R  R  K  F  Y  J  I  T  Y  H  T  S  A  U  L
H  O  T  D  E  N  R  O  I  N  M  N  S  H  L
K  M  N  D  A  E  N  O  A  A  G  V  O  M  A
X  E  O  M  C  Z  S  Z  D  K  M  A  L  T  A
Y  I  Y  I  L  K  A  R  O  B  A  R  O  B  M
R  A  N  B  N  L  I  K  N  P  N  L  S  N  E
C  E  C  O  A  D  Y  P  O  P  H  Y  L  E  L
V  C  Y  W  M  R  U  C  G  E  A  K  E  O  B
L  N  D  R  S  A  C  B  D  B  T  O  D  C  O
T  E  R  U  W  O  H  E  A  R  T  R  A  P  U
G  R  S  U  R  P  Y  C  L  I  A  G  T  Q  R
B  O  U  O  R  B  U  D  I  O  N  J  S  A  N
L  L  M  G  U  O  A  H  O  X  N  D  O  L  E
L  F  H  Z  U  C  A  N  N  E  S  A  C  V  Z
```

*Answers on page 249.*

# CROSS-COUNTRY TRIP

Make your way from coast to coast.

Start

Finish

*Answer on page 249.*

126  123

128
127
129  124 122
130  125
117  118  121

116  115  119 120
114  91  90  89
113  112  111
110  109
132  131
133  108
134  107  106
105
104  103  88  87  67  64
101  102  66  65
100  69  68  63  62

96  97
55
86  85  83  71  60  56  54  52
84  70  61  57  53  49  50
48  45  44  51

161  160
163  159 158  94  98  99  73  74
162  155 157 143 142 141  95  93  33  34
154  151  156  139 140  135 136  16  92  72  75
150  144  138  137  76  77
9  10  78

153  152  82  81  59  58
148  149  80  79  21  47  46  43
164  165  20  22  23  41  42
170  167  18  19  25  24  35
171  166  147  146  37  40  39
31  38
225

172  169  168  6  15  27  32  36
5  13  14  26  28  29  30
174  173  182  183  223  224
1  4  7  8  3  11  177  179  181  222  221
175  2  178  180  186  184  202  220
208  176  193  192  190 188  189  187  185  200  201
210  205  196 191  197  199
209  207  194  195  198  203  219
211  217  206  204
218  215  216  214  213  212

*Answer on page 249.*

# LOOP THE LOOPS MAZE

Loop your way through this maze.

*Answer on page 249.*

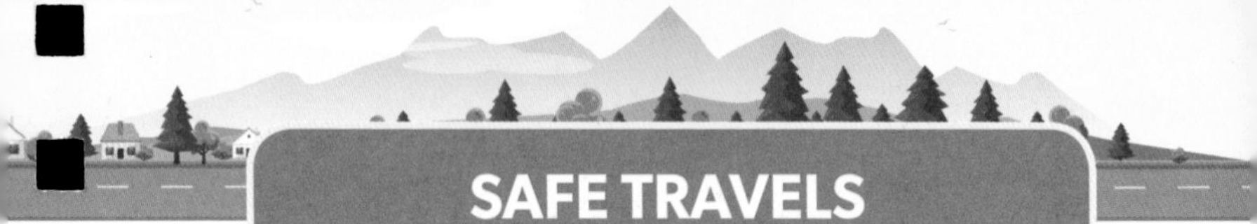

# SAFE TRAVELS

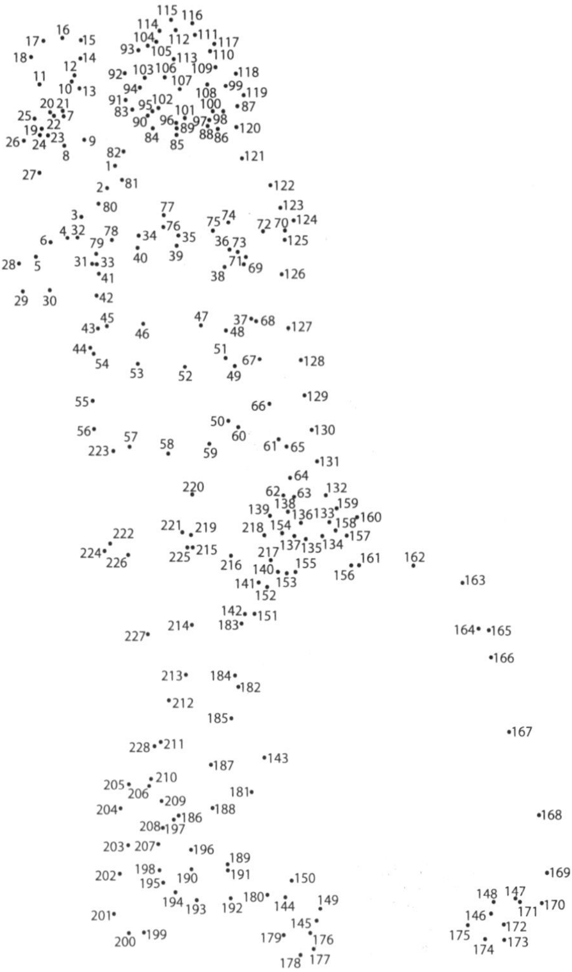

*Answer on page 250.*

# TRAVELING TEAM

Come along with this brother-and-sister team. Finding the 5 changes may turn out to be a real journey!

*Answers on page 250.*

# SUMMER VACATION TIME!

We're *shore* you'll have no trouble landing a list of all 4 of the changes.

**198**

*Answers on page 250.*

# A SANDY SEARCH

We've made some monster-size changes to this scene.
Can you dig up all 4 changes?

*Answers on page 250.*

# SPLASH-TACULAR!

Ride a wave of accomplishment as you find all 5 of these changes.

*Answers on page 251.*

# MANHATTAN

Take a bite out of the Big Apple by finding 5 changes!

# ON THE ROAD AGAIN

Don't pack it in—find all of the 7 changes between these pictures.

*Answers on page 251.*

# COLOSSAL COLOSSEUM

Hunt for all 5 of the ways we've altered this ancient amphitheater.

*Answers on page 251.*

# OLD FAITHFUL FINDER

We're sure you'll gush with excitement once you spot the 4 changes in these photos.

*Answers on page 252.*

Defend your status as a puzzle champ by rooting out all 4 of the changes between these pictures.

*Answers on page 252.*

# SAILING SHENANIGANS

Set sail for fun as you search the
high seas for all 4 of the changes!

*Answers on page 252.*

# UP, UP, AND AWAY!

Some changes have been made to the balloon lineup in each picture. Enjoy the ride as you find 5 changes!

*Answers on page 252.*

# FURRY FRIENDS

We've stuffed this picture with 5 changes.

*Answers on page 253.*

# A MIXED-UP MESS

We're sure you've heard Mom say this before—
if you clean up your act, you should be able
to locate all 8 of the hidden changes!

*Answers on page 253.*

# OFF TO THE BALL GAME

You'll have a ball solving this one,
just be careful and find all 6 changes!

*Answers on page 253.*

# FISH FRENZY

Go out on the prowl for 7 changes
in these underwater scenes.

*Answers on page 253.*

# GOOGLY-EYED GAME

Don't go bug-eyed trying to locate all 6 of the changes in these scenes!

# LINCOLN MEMORIAL

Can you find the 4 puzzling changes that have taken place between these pictures of the Lincoln Memorial?

*Answers on page 254.*

# RED ROCK RIDDLER

Study these pictures closely, and the formation of a list of 6 changes will come to you!

*Answers on page 254.*

# GRAND TETON

Wouldn't it be grand if you found all of the 6 changes between these photos?

*Answers on page 254.*

# BRYCE CANYON

Map the unique terrain at Bryce Canyon while you survey the landscape for 6 changes.

*Answers on page 255.*

# HEARST CASTLE

We've altered one of these palatial estates.
Finding the 5 differences should be enriching.

*Answers on page 255.*

# UNDER THE BRIDGE

Here's a golden opportunity: Find all 4 differences between these spectacular scenes.

*Answers on page 255.*

# PARISIAN PUZZLE

Compare pictures of this world-famous tower
to discover all of 8 the changes we've made.
*Bonne chance!* (Good luck!)

*Answers on page 255.*

# OUT OF THE BLUE

Examine this illuminated city,
and the 8 differences will strike you.

*Answers on page 255.*

# LAS VEGAS

This is the New York-New York Hotel & Casino in Las Vegas. Try your luck at finding all 10 of the differences.

# IMPERIAL ESTATE

Search the photos of this once-forbidden city for 8 changes. Refine your puzzle-solving abilities by investigating these estates.

# THRILLING TASK

We've added a whole carnival of changes to this scene.
Can you find all 7 changes?

*Answers on page 256.*

# ROUND 'EM UP

Can you round up all 7 of the changes
between these pictures?

*Answers on page 256.*

# KNICKKNACK ATTACK

We wouldn't toy with you—we've made
a lot of changes. Can you find all 8?

*Answers on page 256.*

# ANSWER KEY

## It's a Zoo! (page 57)

## Mountains of Fun (page 61)

## Crossword (page 58)

## Loop-de-Loop (page 60)

## U.S. National Parks (page 62)

# ANSWER KEY

## Cartography (page 64)

## Word Ladder (page 66)

Answers may vary.
BAG, bat, bet, JET

## Spin the Dials (page 66)

The word is POCKET.

## Maze-l Tov! (page 67)

## Geo Find It (page 68)

African capitals: Addis Ababa, Kinshasa, Nairobi; Baltic states: Estonia, Latvia, Lithuania; Islands: Cuba, Java, Madagascar; Countries with P names: Pakistan, Peru, Poland; European capitals: Brussels, Kiev, Stockholm

# ANSWER KEY

## Code-doku (page 70)

```
N L E G I T R V A
T R A V E L I N G
G V I R A N E T L
A N G E V R T L I
L E T A N I G R V
R I V L T G N A E
V G N T L E A I R
E T L I R A V G N
I A R N G V L E T
```

## Unusual Places (page 74)

## Going In Circles (page 71)

## More Unusual Places (page 76)

## Geography Riddles (page 72)

## A-maze-ing Race (page 78)

231

# ANSWER KEY

**Gettin' Jiggy (page 79)**
yellow, blue, and pink

**Crossed Words (page 79)**
great/outdoors

**Pretty Fontsy! (page 83)**

**U.S. Landmarks (page 80)**

**Islands (page 84)**
The leftover letters spell:
"Newfoundland."

**About Turn (page 82)**

# ANSWER KEY

## City Find It (page 86)

Cities in Europe: Antwerp, Barcelona, Munich; Cities in Asia: Taipei, Mumbai, Seoul; Cities in North America: Boston, Mexico City, Toronto; Cities in Russia: Moscow, Sochi, St. Petersburg

## Cheese Vision (page 89)

It would seem that B is that best fit, but the answer, when considering the exact angle and shape, is A.

## America A to Z (page 90)

## Spiral Design (page 88)

The spiral in statue A is actually 2 spirals, while the spiral in B is one spiral.

A. 2 spirals

B. 1 double spiral

# ANSWER KEY

## Worldly Food (page 92)

The leftover letters spell: "In addition to crocodile, Australians eat smoked emu, ostrich burgers, camel curry, and cooked kangaroo meats."

## Italy (page 94)

The leftover letters spell: "Italy is one of the great centers of art and fashion."

## City Sites (page 96)

La Scala, Milan; Taj Mahal, Agra; Basin Street, New Orleans; Left Bank, Paris; Colosseum, Rome; Piccadilly Circus, London; Kremlin, Russia; Forbidden City, Beijing; Ginza, Tokyo; Moro Castle, Havana

# ANSWER KEY

### Missing Fs (page 97)

Most people count 6 Fs, but there are actually 8! It's easy to glaze over the Fs in the preposition of—words such as "and," "from," and "of" are processed unconsciously by our mind.

### Mosaic Maze (page 100)

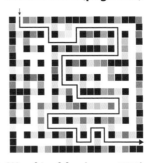

### European Capitals (page 98)

Bucharest; Berlin; Dublin; Copenhagen; Madrid; Budapest; Zagreb; Prague; Athens; Paris; Vienna; Reykjavik; Helsinki; Rome; London; Sofia; Warsaw; Belgrade; Brussels; Lisbon; Amsterdam; Oslo; Tallinn; Valetta

### Word Ladder (page 101)

TRUCK, trick, crick, click, slick, slack, SNACK

### Six Cities to See (page 102)

| C | A | I | R | O | | P | R | A | G | U | E |
|---|---|---|---|---|---|---|---|---|---|---|---|
| A | N | T | I | C | | R | O | L | A | N | D |
| S | T | E | N | T | | I | A | G | R | E | E |
| S | I | N | G | A | P | O | R | E | | | |
| | | | G | E | R | | B | I | G | S | |
| S | E | A | C | O | W | | D | R | A | P | E |
| I | N | C | A | N | | S | E | A | M | A | N |
| S | T | E | M | | A | I | M | | | | |
| | | | B | A | R | C | E | L | O | N | A |
| A | D | O | R | E | R | | R | E | N | A | L |
| D | E | N | I | R | O | | I | N | E | R | T |
| M | O | S | C | O | W | | T | O | K | Y | O |

## Totally Cubular! (page 104)

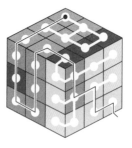

## Countries and Capitals (page 106)

Bonus answers: Buenos Aires, Argentina; Sucre, Bolivia; Brasília, Brazil; Santiago, Chile; Bogotá, Colombia; Quito, Ecuador; Georgetown, Guyana; Asunción, Paraguay; Lima, Peru; Paramaribo, Suriname; Montevideo, Uruguay; Caracas, Venezuela

## Lost City Maze (page 105)

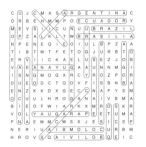

# ANSWER KEY

## Tourist Attractions (page 108)

1. Betsy Ross House
2. Alcatraz Island
3. Empire State Building
4. Epcot Center
5. Franklin Institute
6. Getty Museum
7. Golden Gate Bridge
8. Liberty Bell
9. Willis Tower (was Sears Tower)
10. Space Needle
11. Statue of Liberty
12. White House

## Checkerboard Puzzle (page 109)

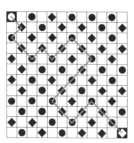

## Around the World (page 110)

## Road Work (page 112)

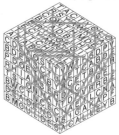

## Word Ladder (page 114)

Answers may vary.
CAMP, came, same, sate, SITE

## Ohio Anagram (page 114)

tooled, Toledo, looted

# ANSWER KEY

## See Your Way Free (page 115)

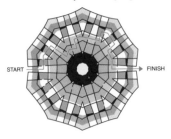

START &rarr;     FINISH

## The State of Things (page 116)

```
F O T O S S C K A A S R H Y I H
A G I U A I R O N L M A K A E V
I H E X C O O A L I A C S N T E
O N E O Y I I N S O U B I N L U
E T D W R S T S I T R A A A A R
N E E I I G I C N L M A D M M K
I N N U A S I E E G L I D O A W
H A O V S N K A N N R I N O T E
A L M I I N A I D U N T V E R S
T L P I O R M F O E A O V A A T
H P A G C O G S L N L E C R E A
I A E S Y H S I A O R A I I D O
A R W W K I I M N M R Z W A H T
O O B A M A E G O I O I V A C O
N T E N I T P N A N A E D H R I
L I P P I I T A A N N I N A S E
```

## Hold Your Tongue! (page 118)

The leftover letters spell: "They speak every language in the world; what are they? Echoes."

```
T H E H H I F U Y P S E
T H A I S L R K P U E A S   A
K E N I A E R V N E R E E     R
Y D L G N A S J S A L V U     A
I O N C I N A E B N I G G     E
P E H N A B N I N E U A U     S
B G I M I A C T T I E I T     E
N A R R P N H N U A H T R     M
N E H A O H A S N R L C O     R
G N J E W M C I I A K I P     U
O G R L E D A T S N E I A     B
W L H S A T A N U R A R S     N
R I E E T H E Y I D E P O     H
E S C E S E N A V A J P S K
H H O R U S S I A N E S
```

## Chopper Lines (page 120)

If you concentrate on the circle that surrounds the lines, the red one appears longer. But, if you concentrate on the helicopters instead, the blue one appears longer. The fact is that the blue is the longest of the pair.

# ANSWER KEY

## Word Ladder (page 121)

HANG, hand, land, lane, line, lime, TIME

HANG
HAND
LAND
LANE
LINE
LIME
TIME

## Asian Anagrams (page 122)

Cambodia; Laos; Armenia; Bhutan; Brunei; Bangladesh; China; North Korea; Mongolia; Taiwan; India; Thailand; Vietnam; Sri Lanka; Indonesia; South Korea; Singapore; Pakistan; Nepal; Iran; Myanmar; Malaysia; Israel; Philippines

## South America Scramble (page 124)

Colombia; Machu Picchu; Inca; Ecuador; rain forest; football; deforestation; Amazon River; La Paz; Argentina; Rio de Janeiro; Spanish; Andes; Portuguese; Bolivia; Venezuela

# ANSWER KEY

## African Adventure (page 126)

| H | A | T | C | H | | F | A | I | N | T |
|---|---|---|---|---|---|---|---|---|---|---|
| O | M | A | H | A | | A | D | R | A | W |
| K | I | L | I | M | A | N | J | A | R | O |
| U | N | C | | M | L | S | | N | C | O |
| M | O | S | D | E | F | | L | I | O | N |
| | | | E | R | R | E | D | | | |
| O | R | Y | X | | E | A | S | T | E | R |
| R | E | E | | A | D | S | | H | R | E |
| B | U | S | H | C | U | I | S | I | N | E |
| I | N | O | U | T | | E | L | C | I | D |
| T | E | R | M | S | | R | A | K | E | S |

## Types of Maps (page 128)

| L | A | C | I | T | U | A | N | K | M | L | P | N |
|---|---|---|---|---|---|---|---|---|---|---|---|---|
| P | R | C | I | H | P | A | R | G | O | P | O | T |
| O | S | N | Q | T | I | M | E | Z | O | N | E | T |
| L | P | T | H | K | A | O | R | E | L | I | E | F |
| I | T | K | R | I | Q | M | J | Q | H | V | U | M |
| T | T | B | N | E | G | O | E | L | H | T | U | A |
| I | Y | E | R | D | E | Y | A | H | R | S | N | R |
| C | Y | X | J | F | O | T | V | H | T | H | N | G |
| A | M | L | A | C | I | G | O | L | O | E | G | O |
| L | A | C | I | S | Y | H | P | I | T | Z | L | T |
| E | M | G | B | K | A | T | L | A | S | D | O | R |
| V | Q | C | L | I | M | A | C | T | I | C | B | A |
| K | T | Z | S | W | E | A | T | H | E | R | E | C |

## Roll the Dice (page 130)

Even though the red dot on the farther die seems much larger, it is the exact same size as the red dot on the closer die. The illusion is a trick of perception.

## United States Geographic Trivia (page 131)

1. The four corners of Utah, Colorado, New Mexico, and Arizona
2. Missouri and Tennessee each border 8 other states
3. Yes
4. Wyoming is north of Colorado
5. Maine

# ANSWER KEY

## African Anagrams (page 132)

Uganda; Ghana; Sudan; Mauritania; Burkina Faso; Benin; Cameroon; Cape Verde; Burundi; Togo; Djibouti; Tunisia; Malawi; Mali; Madagascar; Angola; Gabon; Ethiopia; Niger; Sierra Leone; Senegal; Seychelles; Botswana; Eritrea; Equatorial Guinea; Rwanda

## Got Hot (page 135)

1. got hot; 2. cub snub; 3. slow flow; 4. dorm form; 5. finer liner; 6. rift shift; 7. muddy study; 8. reach beach; 9. stock shock; 10. regal eagle

## Traveling in Style (page 136)

## U.S. Trivia (page 134)

1. Ohio
2. Yes, Rhode Island
3. In the Carolinas, in Indiana, in Idaho, and in Maryland
4. Q
5. Alabama

# ANSWER KEY

### Least Populous Places
(page 138)

### Five International Cities
(page 140)

| M | A | S | K | S | | M | A | C | A | U |
|---|---|---|---|---|---|---|---|---|---|---|
| A | C | H | A | T | | A | T | A | L | L |
| K | U | A | L | A | L | U | M | P | U | R |
| E | T | D | | B | E | L | | E | M | I |
| R | E | S | A | L | E | | M | R | S | C |
| | | | M | E | C | C | A | | | |
| B | A | T | S | | H | A | R | H | A | R |
| E | C | H | | P | E | R | | O | R | O |
| B | U | E | N | O | S | A | I | R | E | S |
| O | R | I | O | N | | T | A | S | T | E |
| P | A | R | I | S | | S | N | E | E | S |

### Circle Takes the Square
(page 142)

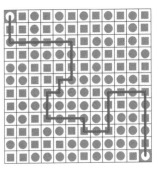

### Totally Cube-ular!
(page 143)
A and B

242

# ANSWER KEY

## The Bahamas (page 144)

The leftover letters spell: "The Bahamas include two thousand cays and seven hundred islands."

## Word Ladder (page 146)

SEEK, seed, send, mend, mind, FIND

SEEK
SEED
SEND
MEND
MIND
FIND

## Space Race (page 147)

## In Switzerland (page 148)

| | | | | | | | | | |
|---|---|---|---|---|---|---|---|---|---|
| A | L | P | S | ■ | U | L | T | R | A |
| L | E | O | I | ■ | S | O | R | E | L |
| L | A | K | E | G | E | N | E | V | A |
| S | N | E | V | A | ■ | I | B | E | T |
| ■ | ■ | ■ | E | O | S | ■ | E | R | E |
| L | A | N | D | L | O | C | K | E | D |
| I | T | E | ■ | S | B | A | ■ | ■ | ■ |
| T | E | S | S | ■ | E | T | H | I | C |
| M | A | T | T | E | R | H | O | R | N |
| U | S | O | U | R | ■ | E | S | A | U |
| S | E | R | B | S | ■ | R | E | N | T |

## State Birds (page 150)

# ANSWER KEY

## Up and Over (page 152)

## 90 Degrees (page 153)

There are 8 angles. Most people locate 6, though there are 2 deceptive angles hidden between the houses. Some of the angles may not look like right angles, but this due to a trick of apparent perspective.

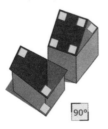

## Brazil (page 154)

The leftover letters spell: "The spectacular annual festival of carnival is one of the greatest shows on Earth."

```
T H O R I E N A J E D O I R E
S P O P O S S U M E C T A A C
C U L L A P O R T U G U E S E
R A P A R R O T S M G A M L N
N C R I E U A B L A H T O L S
F I R N V E S R J C T B U A I
V R E S I A L A O A F O N F C
A E T R R V P S N W S S T U I
A M A Z O N A I I V A S A C A
O A E L C I R L S O M A I A O
C H T N O E D I P O B N N U F
E T N T N L O A P H A O S G E
L U A G I R U E U A T V E I S
O O T F R L S H M O W A S O N
T S E R O F N I A R E A R T H
```

## Vacation Destinations (page 156)

```
D L R O W A E S S E A S I D E
I L A N E D G L A S V E G A S
R S J E E D T T I P C E A G
X U D I K M O B G U E N T O K
N Y O N B B L D D R H L N R N
A L T A U I Q O C A V A D S
E R B A O L K H V N I P E O N
B U E A K C S F T T L I N O E
B O R T C E E I W A I Q A W D
I T M O L N C C N A Q S R Y R
R D U T P C X O W I O M R L A
A L D S I E A T O G A E L G
C R A T S T H S T T I R T O H
R O Y N A D E T N N A N I H C
A W V N Q P A D F S U G D V S
D I S N E Y W O R L D O E P U
S L L A F A R A G A I N M M B
Q W H K N E W Y O R K C I T Y
T A B Z S Y E K A D I R O L F
P I R T G N I P M A C A N N R
```

244

# ANSWER KEY

## Maze (page 158)

## Rhyme Time (page 159)

1. fair share; 2. cool school; 3. blast past; 4. clean teen; 5. pack snack; 6. square chair; 7. calf's laughs; 8. finer diner; 9. loco cocoa; 10. slower mower; 11. stole coal

## Road Trip (page 160)

## City Nicknames (page 162)

## Country Balloons (page 164)

1. Peru, U; 2. Kenya, A; 3. India, I; 4. Japan, A; 5. Egypt, T; 6. Spain, S; 7. Korea, A; 8. Brazil, R; 9. England, L
Bonus country: Australia

## Geography Scramblegram (page 165)

# ANSWER KEY

## Card Games (page 166)

## Word Ladder (page 168)

PLANE, plant, plait, plain, blain, brain, TRAIN

## Square Holdings (page 169)

## Cross Country (page 170)

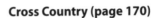

## Diagonal Jump (page 171)

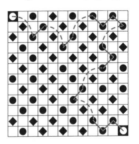

## African Capitals (page 172)

# ANSWER KEY

## Old Names (page 174)

1. Bangladesh; 2. Belize;
3. Ethiopia; 4. Haiti;
5. Ghana; 6. Iran; 7. Iraq;
8. Istanbul; 9. Kenya;
10. Mali; 11. Myanmar;
12. New York City; 13. Sri
Lanka; 14. Thailand;
15. Zimbabwe

## France (page 178)

The leftover letters spell:
"France is sometimes
referred to as 'the hexagon'
because of the geometric
shape of its territory."

## On the Map (page 176)

## Copyrights (page 180)

They are all the same size.
This illusion is known as an
Ebbinghaus illusion.

# ANSWER KEY

## Traffic Tango (page 181)

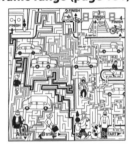

## Popular Attractions (page 182)

## Geographagrams (page 184)

1. LAOS
2. CHINA
3. YEMEN
4. ITALY
5. MALI
6. OMAN
7. SPAIN
8. NEPAL
9. PERU
10. IRAN
11. ALGERIA
12. ISRAEL

## Pyramid Lines (page 185)

Yes.

## Star Contrast (page 186)

Yes.

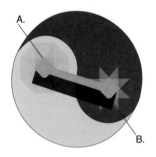

## A Capital Puzzle! (page 187)

1. Lansing (MI);
2. Topeka (KS);
3. Denver (CO);
4. Salem (OR);
5. Boston (MA)

# ANSWER KEY

## Florida (page 188)

## City Skyline (page 193)

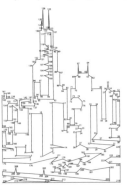

## Exotic Travel (page 190)

## Loop the Loops Maze (page 194)

## Cross-Country Trip (page 192)

# ANSWER KEY

## Safe Travels (page 195)

## Summer Vacation Time!
*(page 198)*

## Traveling Team
*(pages 196–197)*

## A Sandy Search *(page 199)*

# ANSWER KEY

### ■Splash-tacular! *(page 200)*

### ■On the Road Again *(page 202)*

### ■Manhattan *(page 201)*

### ■Colossal Colosseum *(page 203)*

# ANSWER KEY

**■Old Faithful Finder** *(page 204)*

**■Sailing Shenanigans**
*(pages 206–207)*

**■The Alamo** *(page 205)*

**■Up, Up, and Away!** *(page 208)*

# ANSWER KEY

■**Furry Friends** *(page 209)*

■**Off to the Ball Game** *(page 211)*

■**A Mixed-Up Mess** *(page 210)*

■**Fish Frenzy** *(page 212)*

253

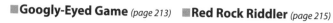

# ANSWER KEY

**■ Googly-Eyed Game** *(page 213)*

**■ Red Rock Riddler** *(page 215)*

**■ Lincoln Memorial** *(page 214)*

**■ Grand Teton** *(page 216)*

# ANSWER KEY

## ■Bryce Canyon *(page 217)*

## ■Parisian Puzzle *(pages 220–221)*

## ■Hearst Castle *(page 218)*

## ■Under the Bridge *(page 219)*

## ■Out of the Blue
*(page 222)*

# ANSWER KEY

## ■Las Vegas *(page 223)*

## ■Thrilling Task *(page 226)*

## ■Imperial Estate *(pages 224–225)*

## ■Round 'em Up! *(page 227)*

## ■Knickknack Attack *(page 228)*